The Kindergarten Book

A Guide to Literacy Instruction

Marilyn Duncan

Illustrations by Joanne Friar

Richard C. Owen Publishers, Inc.
Katonah, New York

"Characteristics of Learners (Emergent through Early 1)" in Appendix C from *Literacy Learning: Teachers as Professional Decision Makers.* © 2004 by Margaret E. Mooney. Reprinted by permission.

"Words I Know" from *Readers as Writers and Writers as Readers: Creating a Reading/Writing Folder* by Margaret E. Mooney, Figure 5. © 2004 by Margaret E. Mooney.

The "Essential Word List" in Chapter 3 adapted from *Spell-Write: An Aid to Writing and Spelling* by Cedric Croft, pages 32–34. © 1998 by New Zealand Council for Educational Research. Reprinted by permission.

"Monitoring Letters, Sounds, and Words" in Appendix B, "The Literacy Record" front and back in Chapter 3 and Appendix D, "Templates for Student Planning Sheets" in Appendix F, "Monthly Plan" in Appendix G, "Weekly Plan" in Appendix H, and "Teacher Daily Plan" in Appendix I © 2005 by Marilyn Duncan. Permission is granted for teachers to make photocopies of the forms in this book for classroom use only.

My Book text © 2005 by Marilyn Duncan. Illustrations © 2005 by Joanne Friar.

The "Essential Skills" in Chapter 8 from *The New Zealand Curriculum Framework,* page 17, © 1993 by Ministry of Education of New Zealand.

The "Student Daily Plan Icons" in Appendix F © 2005 by Joanne Friar. Permission is granted for teachers to make photocopies of the icons in this book for classroom use only.

The Fox text © 1996 by Janice Boland.

My Dog Fuzzy text © 2001 by Janice Boland. Illustrations © 2001 by Philip Smith.

Bedtime text © 2001 by Amy J. Finney. Illustrations © 2001 by Marilyn Mets.

The names of all the students in this book have been changed to respect their privacy.

Library of Congress Cataloging-in-Publication Data
Duncan, Marilyn.
    The kindergarten book : a guide to literacy instruction / Marilyn Duncan ; illustrations by Joanne Friar.
        p. cm.
    Summary: "Describes how kindergarten teachers can better plan for and teach literacy through careful observation and assessment of students and a deep understanding of their development as learners. Includes planning and monitoring forms"—Provided by publisher.
    Includes bibliographical references and index.
    ISBN-13: 978-1-57274-704-3 (13-digit pbk.)
    ISBN-10: 1-57274-704-8 (10-digit pbk.)
  1. Reading (Kindergarten) 2. Language arts (Kindergarten) I. Title.
    LB1181.2D86 2005
    372.4—dc22   2005008760

Richard C. Owen Publishers, Inc.
PO Box 585
Katonah, NY 10536
914-232-3903; 914-232-3977 fax
www.RCOwen.com

Acquisitions Editor: Darcy H. Bradley   *Cover Design:* Damian Powers
Production Manager: Amy J. Finney / Phyllis Morrison   *Back Cover Photography:* Ron Whitfield
Printed in the United States of America

9 8 7 6 5 4 3 2 1

To Jan
... who was the shadow of the reader
on the shoulder of this writer
from the beginning to the end.

table of contents

preface

The purpose of this book is to encourage a conversation between the reader and the author about why and how to move students along a continuum of literacy in kindergarten. *The Kindergarten Book* addresses questions about the kindergarten teacher's role in literacy learning. The book is based on a set of beliefs about literacy and teaching and learning that are critical to the effective professional development of teachers of young children.

For those of us with experience of kindergarten teaching, this book illustrates how beliefs become the foundation for understanding about learning and teaching.

- Learning occurs best when it is built on learner's strengths, when we determine what the learner can do, what the learner is attempting to do, and then decide what we need to do next.
- Learning is developmental; as the more knowledgeable other, we develop readers, writers, mathematicians, and thinkers along a continuum of development.
- Every learner has unlimited potential, and it is our job to realize and release that potential.
- Personal reflection is the key to developing our own learning. Our ability to ask questions of ourselves allows us to make shifts in what we do, and why and how we do it.

The book begins with an introduction. The reader is invited to walk through a kindergarten classroom seven months into the school year. Chapter 1 explores what a teacher needs to understand about the development of a literacy set for kindergarten children. Chapter 2 provides examples of how a kindergarten teacher gathers relevant information about the incoming students, and how the information is valued to determine what individual children know and what they need to know next. Three children are introduced in this chapter as case studies to be followed more closely through the book.

Chapter 3 explores the tools used to monitor literacy learning growth. Chapter 4 discusses organizing the environment to support literacy learning, and Chapter 5 provides guidance in how the environment is introduced in the first weeks of school. Chapter 6 focuses on scheduling the teacher's time to manage learning.

Teaching for learning is explored in Chapter 7, with an emphasis on how to use the child as a guide to instruction. Chapter 8 describes the support needed for children to progress through the emergent stage of the literacy continuum. Chapter 9 provides examples of how knowledge and skills are developed as children move into the early stage of the literacy continuum.

The book ends with Chapter 10, which returns to the author's beliefs that were introduced above. The book concludes by revisiting the three case study children to explore their progress seven months into the school year.

acknowledgments

I was introduced to the teaching world by watching my mother as I grew up. She showed me that teaching is an honorable profession, that children have the right to an interesting classroom, that learning is what is supposed to happen, and that it all takes a great deal of work. Thank you for providing such a wonderful model. I was raised in an atmosphere of positive potential. I believed that anything was possible for me because of my mother and father. You two are loved.

I have many others to acknowledge for their contribution to the thinking that inspired this book. To Dorothy Yamashita, who long ago in Hawaii showed me the importance of watching children and the magic of the development of the five year old. To Jeannie Davis, Jackie Graef, Marolyn Haws, Karen Herzog, Debbie Shelton, Stephanie Tennille, and Anne Thiebeau for the opportunity to experience both congeniality and collegiality as we worked. To Larry Bauer and Kent Davis for being the kind of administrators who looked at innovation in teaching as something to encourage, not harness.

Thank you to Kay Coleman and Debbie Backus, administrators who value learning above all for teachers, children, and other administrators. To Bonnie Rhodes, there is no doubt that my favorite years of teaching were the ones when the door was always ajar between our rooms. To Mike Shelton (Mom always liked you best) for always asking me the right questions.

I owe a huge debt of gratitude to The Learning Network®. Thank you to Richard Owen who had a vision of what is possible in education and began to bring together people who were willing to work to make the vision a reality. To my coordinator colleagues, I relish the times when I am able to learn with you. You work harder than any educators I know to figure out how to best support schools, teachers, and children. I appreciate the tenacity of Dianne Kotaska, Dottie Kirby, Katie Moeller, and Mary Ann Whitfield to maintain the consistency of what we do best while always searching for ways to do it better. I thank Phyllis Greenspan for knowing when to laugh and when to listen.

This book would have never been written if I had not spent time in the classrooms of many gifted kindergarten teachers. For always allowing me to be there, ask questions, and learn from you and your children, I am indebted to: Jill Tinker, Dawn Gillespie, and Karolee Hess; Cindy Brown, Peggy Moses, Kris Hase, and Jane Lapointe. For the rich conversations about young children that continued to change and reframe my beliefs, I thank David and Angela Matteson. A special thank you goes to Charlene Graham who shared her kindergarten class with me and continued to collect data each time I asked for it.

I depended upon Sharon Martel to keep me honest. She shared her opinions, asked the hard questions, and provided feedback and encouragement. She kept me in the kindergarten classroom when I couldn't physically be there.

The following people provided their insight and expertise to help ensure this book would make sense and be helpful to kindergarten teachers anywhere. I respect and appreciate the time and efforts of Dr. Jo Ann Brewer, Terry Botsford, Nancy Creech, Kaye Marshall, and Sara Latterman.

Thank you to Darcy Bradley, the best editor a writer could have. You knew when to call, when to push, and when to be quiet. You have a gift of challenging and supporting at the same time. Thanks to Amy J. Finney, whose expertise makes everything look just the way I imagined it could, and to Phyllis Morrison for her attention to detail.

Special gratitude goes to Phoebe Duncan, Andy Duncan, Ivy Duncan, and Oshyn Nobmann, whose attitudes and understandings about life and learning continually remind me that all children deserve great teachers.

Thanks to Chad and Heidi, who have grown up to be the best friends any mother could ask for and who have provided the inspiration for many of the stories in this book.

And finally, thank you to my husband, Peter Duncan, who was willing to drop anything he was doing to listen, read, ask questions, revise, encourage, and convince me that I knew enough to finish this book. I am forever blessed that you have come into my life.

introduction   a day in the life of a kindergarten classroom

It's just an ordinary day, a little more than half way through the school year. The room is empty, but it is obvious this is the work place for five and six year olds. There are places to meet, places where children work in small groups, and places for children to work individually. I look at the student work on the walls—artwork created with paint, construction paper, and other bits and pieces. The science area is literally alive with a resident turtle, a small aquarium, and a guinea pig. Content area books are on a table to support investigating the treasures of five year olds—the bits and pieces that arrived in backpacks and pockets: Rocks and sticks, leaves and flowers, and the contents of an old watch sit alongside magnifying glasses and tweezers.

There is an area for children to listen to stories on tape, and their favorite selections are hanging nearby in plastic bags. One bookshelf has alphabet puzzles and games and other opportunities to work with words. A flannel board with puppets occupies one corner of the classroom library. Pillows and beanbag chairs look inviting. Trade books and the children's own published books are available for reading. Each table has a basket filled with books that students write in every day. Even before the children arrive it is obvious that learning is occurring in this room.

I am pleased as I look at the differences in the writing of these children. I see sketches of segmented bodies at the tops of pages, where earlier in the year legs came directly out of heads. I read what they have written. Some of the stories are entertaining and quite easy to read. Others contain approximations of words. I can make sense of them with the aid of the picture. A few are made up of letters or letter-like symbols that only make sense to me when I remember what the child had been talking about.

Writing is not the only change that has occurred since the beginning of the school year. I remember wondering how long it would take for children to become less dependent. There were children who didn't say a word and children who talked all the time. There were some who would rather sit under the table, or on it, than in the chairs around it. I was supporting 23 children, four different languages, and a wide range of experiences. This class of children was more diverse than any I had previously experienced.

I glance at the clock, grab a small notebook and pencil, and walk toward the kindergarten playground for a few minutes before the school day begins. I hear the noise of children before I reach the outside door. These kindergarteners come in different shapes, sizes, and appearances. One common theme, however, is that they are delighted to see me, and the chatter directed at me is instantaneous.

"Guess what? I got new shoes last night!"
"Wow, they look like they'll help you run and climb."

"You should see my big owie. I fell on the sidewalk in front of my house last night and my mom had to get the rocks out of my knee!"
"Whew! I would have yelled if that had happened to me!"

"Hi, Sophie. I bet you remembered to bring your library book back."
Sophie nods and points to her backpack.
"I knew you would!"

"Jose, how do you spell the word *it*?"
Jose responds with a twinkle in his eye. *"I-T!"*
"Good for you! Now you can read and write that word every day."

"Can you tie my shoe?"
"Why don't you start, and I'll help when you need it?"
Dani ties her shoe.
"Hey—you don't need me at all!"

"My Nana and Tata are coming on one more day after today."
"So if today is Tuesday, what day will that be?"
"Wednesday!"
"You'll be really excited to see them on Wednesday. Do you have plans for what you'll do when they're here?"
"They're going to take me to the park and my Nana is going to make tamales and my Tata is going to play soccer with me. He taught my Daddy to play soccer when he was the same size as me."
"While they're visiting, you'll have a lot to write about." Julio smiles and runs to the slide.

I look at my notebook. By Colin's name, I have written: new shoes. Next to Jasmine, I have written: skinned knee. By Dani, I have written: tie shoes. Next to Julio, I have written: grandparents' visit. I raise my hand, and the children line up and make their way with me to the classroom.

It's business as usual as we cross through the door. The children unload their backpacks and place them on hooks with their sweaters and jackets. They put books back in boxes that have their names on them. Papers that need to be returned are placed in labeled baskets. On a wall chart with names and photographs, children are turning over their cards that tell me they are at school today. Library books are returned to the classroom bookshelves or to a labeled library books basket. I think how independent these children have become in four and a half months.

Quiet conversation is occurring. They talk about what they expect to do during this first block of time in the classroom. The children begin their work and they start their daily planning. I begin by completing the necessary daily paperwork, talking with a few parents, and then I get to work.

I ask Janisha what she plans to do this morning. She says, "See, I'm going to read first." She places a number one in a box with a picture of a book. "Then I'm going to practice spelling." She has put a number two by a picture of a sheet of paper with a list of words. "I'll go to the puppets and flannel boards to tell stories." Number three is placed next to a corresponding picture. "And then I'll write." Janisha's plan is shown in Figure 1. As I look around the room, I see the other children either working on their student plan or busy on their first task.

I am busy as well. At this time, I gather information about my students' progress. I look at my own plan to see whose reading I will be monitoring today. I sit alongside Quentin. He is reading a small book about a gecko, and I record his oral reading. I hand him a book he has not seen before, and I record how he reads that book as well. I place both records in a folder to analyze later in the day.

While I am working with individual students, the other children are busy all over the room. I can be confident that their activity is purposeful and focused on their literacy learning. Some children are writing. Some are on the floor of the classroom library reading aloud. A few are sitting at tables with white boards and markers, practicing how to write high frequency words. Some are telling familiar stories with the aid of flannel board characters and a flannel board. A few are on the floor with alphabet puzzles. I move quietly about the room after I finish with each child and check in with certain students. I note the changes in how they work in the classroom. For example, Alberto no longer asks what to do next; when he finishes a task he easily makes a decision about what he will do next. Sophie is more outspoken about the character she will portray at the flannel board. Maria and Paul are spending more time at the book area with books and both show interest in the books they have previously read in small groups.

The classroom library is a hub of activity this morning. Colin is reading aloud from a book he has written, "I had a soccer game last Saturday. I made a goal. It was a close game, but we won!" He looks at Nina sitting beside him and adds, "We did win! My goal made the score 4 to 3!"

name: _Janisha_   date: 8/7/

Monday   Tuesday   Wednesday   Thursday   (Friday)

| 1 | 2 | 3 | 4 | 5 | 6 | 7 | 8 |

reading

writing

word work

handrwiting

listening

spelling

investigation

storytelling

Figure 1: Janisha's Student Plan

Nina nods and continues to read her book selection, *Dogs at School* (Hardin 1999). She is laughing as she reads quietly. Nina is becoming a more sophisticated reader. I ask her what's so funny. "Max and Toby are being bad again," she says. I learn that this is the second book she has read about these dogs; she highlights the dog trouble in the first book. "See what I mean?" she says, pointing to a line of text that reads, "Dogs don't go to school, but Max and Toby went inside with the children." Another book in this series could be a good match for her. I make a note to find that book for her.

Julio is sitting with his draft writing book open in front of him. "I can see you're writing about the visit from your Nana and Tata, Julio." He nods with a big smile. "It's going to be fun when they're here. Tell me about your plan."

Julio talks about his parents picking him up from school and how they will drive straight to the airport. He talks about having dinner with his grandparents when they get back to his house. I comment that it sounds as if he has several things to write about. I remind him of the writing I have been doing in front of the class and show him how I divided my plan into parts so the story can be about more than one thing. (See Figure 2.)

Figure 2: Writing Demonstration

Julio draws a few lines after his initial sketch. "I'll put the driving part here," he says, "and the airport part will go here." He points to the second box. "Then I'll need one more place for the dinner part."

"Now you'll remember all the important things," I reply. "I think your Nana and Tata will be so excited to read this when it's published."

I see that it's time to bring the group together. I quietly sing at the front of the room and sit in a chair beside a large easel. The children begin singing along as they leave what they are doing and come to the floor. I smile at the ease of these transitions, remembering the consistent practice it took right from the beginning to make this happen.

I hold up a picture book. "I've read that book before!" Kyle states.

"Some books we love hearing more than once," I reply.

Many children nod in agreement. I talk about how books give you information and can answer your questions and why I like to choose books like that. I mention questions I have about guinea pigs because there are some things I am wondering. (Several students provide answers. I continue to talk.)

"I found this book in the library this morning in the section that is called non-fiction. That's the place you find books that give you information. I looked in the section that has the animal books. I chose this book because I liked the photographs on the front cover."

I don't talk down to these five year olds, but bring clarity through the language and examples I use. I point to the large print on the cover. "This is the title. It says, *Care for Your Guinea Pig* (Hearne 1981). Because the guinea pig on the cover looks like our guinea pig, Oreo, I thought the author might know the answers to some questions I have."

I turn to the title page. "The first thing I do is remember my question, 'Where should a guinea pig live?' I need to look for places in the book that might answer that question."

I begin reading, stopping every once in awhile to make some comments about the text that supports what I know about guinea pigs and how I learned it. The children comment during my reading, as well; they are learning that I am not distracted. Their talk is evidence of their engagement in the instruction. As I turn the pages, I continue to think aloud about the questions I am asking.

"OHhhhhh..." is the response from the children as the page is turned and they see a picture of a guinea pig hutch.

"I can tell you are thinking what I'm thinking! Here's a picture that shows a place for guinea pigs to live. And look at this. The bold print at the top of the page says 'The Hutch!' I think a hutch must be that cage in the picture. That gives me a hint that my question is going to be answered on this page."

I continue to read, talking about how I am finding the answer, and how this fits with what I know a guinea pig needs. I quickly read through the rest of the book, remarking only a few more times on what I find interesting.

"This book gave me the answer to my question, but it did something else. It made me ask myself some more questions about guinea pigs that I would like to know how to answer. I wonder if any of you have questions as well. Hey, I have an idea!"

I turn to a chart that is hanging nearby on the wall. "I think I'm going to add a new topic to my topic list for writing. Hmmm... what should I write up there? Let me see. I know. Questions and answers about guinea pigs!"

I write this topic on my list, shown in Figure 3. Some topics are crossed off; some are waiting to be written.

Figure 3: Topic List

"I have another idea. I'm going to put a piece of paper over by Oreo's cage. I'll divide it into boxes like this. That way we can write other questions we might have in each of the boxes as we look at our guinea pig. Let me write the one I was wondering about when I finished the book."

I jot down the question, "What food besides lettuce should Oreo eat?"

"I'll leave this marker over here so you can write the questions you might have too. I think we'll find some of the answers in books, but I also think we might find some answers by just observing our guinea pig and how she lives in her hutch."

I stand and begin to recite a poem. The children stand and join in. We finish with some familiar poems and songs. The last one ends with the children sitting on the floor. I begin to talk about the writing I started the day before.

"If you remember, I was writing about running out of dishwasher soap at my house. I need to look at my plan and see what I intended to write and see if I anything is left out."

I check the sketches drawn in four boxes across the top of my plan, shown in Figure 2. I add more to the last two sketches and talk about where my writing is going to go today.

"I'd better re-read what I have written so far, so I know where to start. Let's see. Those check marks in the first two boxes remind me that I have already written about these two parts of the story." I want to make sure I haven't left anything important out. I read, "Darn! I forgot to get dishwasher soap at the store. I have an idea. I'll use laundry soap."

I recheck my plan to see if I left anything out then continue talking. "I need to add today's date to know where I started today." I write 3/8 on the chart. I add, "Now it's important that I get this part just right because this is where the problem started." (See Figure 4.)

I read my story again. "Darn! I forgot to get dishwasher soap at the store. I have an idea. I'll use laundry soap." Then I add, "That will work!" I continue, "I think I need to say why I think that will work." I continue to write, "After all, soap is soap, right?" I stop and smile. "I like how that sounds... 'soap is soap, right?' "

I write and talk a little longer, then stop and look at the children. "That's all I can do today, but I can tell you know the best part will come tomorrow."

Figure 4: Writing Demonstration Continued

The children are buzzing with comments about what they think will happen. I ask them to turn to the person next to them and talk about what they were doing before they came to the front of the room and what they expect to do next. I walk among the students listening to them talk and make a few comments or suggestions here and there. I tap pairs of children on the shoulder and suggest they get back to work. Soon the room is a hum of activity. Once again, children are reading, writing, talking, listening, observing, and learning.

My daily plan reminds me to check in with Celeste to see how she is practicing the learning of new words. I stand behind her and watch her work. I want to see how she is applying what we have been working on. She looks at the word "in" in the spelling notebook in front of her. I hear her say the word—"in." I watch her close her eyes and softly say each letter of the word—"I-N." Then I watch her write the word "in."

"Are you right?" I lean over and ask her.

"Yes!" she replies, pointing to each letter in the word.
"See—i-n—just like in my spelling notebook."

"Good for you!" I comment.

I bring a few children to the floor for a reading group. We sit on the floor in a circle and talk about what we expect to read in this book. The children read. We talk in this small group about what the author wants us to understand about this book. We use the pictures, words, and our thinking to help us make sense of the text. I look for the challenges children are experiencing with the meaning of the book, with letters, sounds, and words, and I provide support where needed to overcome those challenges. We talk about what we might have added or taken away from the book if we had been the writers. We work together for about ten minutes before the children return to what they were doing and I move about the room.

The rest of our language arts block continues this way. I sit alongside children who are writing and record their work in a small blank book. I talk about their stories, the letters, the sounds, spaces between words, and the different skills these writers need as I work alongside them.

As children complete the tasks they are required to do, they begin others. Some practice handwriting and play word games. Others observe the guinea pig and write down questions. A few are lying on the floor, reading big books and using pointers to read charts and poetry. There are students who dramatize stories they know in the puppet and storytelling area. They talk with each other about their experiences.

The pattern of my day is to move in and out of working with individuals, small groups, and the whole class. My day is not filled with presenting a series of lessons to the whole class. Instead my day is determined by how I scheduled my time, based upon what I know my students can do and need to do next.

As you experienced this day in a kindergarten classroom, what did you wonder as a teacher of five and six year olds? Did you think about what the potential is for readers and writers at this age? Can children read and write who don't know the names of letters and the sounds they make? Why would a teacher write each day in front of the kindergarten children? Were you concerned about "pushing" these children? How do you reconcile new ideas with what you currently do in your classroom? How willing are you to think about making changes in your classroom practice?

Change is often presented to us through the latest new method, program, or the next quick fix. The problem with methodological solutions—finding the best way to teach reading and writing in kindergarten—is that they often fail to address the right questions.

Methodological solutions focus on how to teach reading and writing, but the more appropriate question is, "How do we develop readers and writers?" This thinking is a significant change in the way the teacher's role is defined. The role shifts from being an expert in the teaching of reading and writing as subjects to being a teacher of young learners who are already on a continuum of becoming readers and writers.

Teaching that begins with becoming readers and writers also begins with questions about where our students are along the literacy learning continuum, how we find out and what we do when we know. This perspective on teaching causes us to reflect on what we know about ourselves as learners, and what we know about ourselves as teachers. To many experienced teachers this may be a change in perspective. We may be used to making changes because someone has told us to change, because a new program has been purchased, or because we went to a workshop and got more ideas.

Kindergarten teachers who reflect on their teaching practices are open to making significant changes in how they practice their craft. Reflection often begins with a simple challenge. When what we are doing doesn't seem to be working, or could be working better, we begin to ask questions. Changes begin when we look for answers to our questions; when we match what we know about young children and literacy development with what we are expected to achieve and what we know children can achieve. We grow as teachers—as learners—when new understandings drive changes to our practice.

1   the literacy set

Language is a tool for learning. Language is central to intellectual, social, and emotional development. Through language the learner shares knowledge, experiences, information, ideas, and feelings. Children experience the effects of language by listening, talking, and observing long before they enter school.

INTERRELATEDNESS OF LANGUAGE MODES

Children receive language by listening, viewing, and reading. They produce language by speaking, presenting, and writing. These language modes are interactive and interrelated. Children make sense of their world through the interaction of these language modes.

A child in the classroom library reading *Jesse Bear, What Will You Wear?* (Carlstrom 1986) uses the same intonation as her teacher used when reading the story to the class. She is interpreting the meaning orally. A child who draws a picture about losing a tooth begins to write the story below the picture using the sounds and letters he knows. A child listening to the administrator on the intercom points to the speaker in the ceiling and says, "Miss Hess must have to lie down up there when she's talking!"

Though interrelated, examples of the language modes are referred to independently throughout this chapter. The purpose of this separation is to recognize the distinct characteristics of each, and throughout the rest of the book the reader is invited to assume their interrelatedness.

THE LITERACY SET

Children enter kindergarten from a variety of cultural, social, and economic backgrounds. They also come with a variety of experiences and are naturally curious, with many questions. Natural curiosity and experimentation are part of being a child.

Many children have limited literacy experiences before school entry, but rich experiences with learning. They are talkers, bike riders, door openers, and juice pourers. They are enthusiastic about knowing something new. They have been learning since birth.

What children have learned prior to coming to school provides evidence of what they understand about literacy. Children who begin school with significant experiences in reading and writing typically become high progress readers and writers (Adams 1990; Clay 1991; Holdaway 1979; Wells 1985). They are more likely to demonstrate the expected behaviors of beginning readers or writers. Influenced by rich early literacy experiences, they have positive attitudes and a developing understanding of how books, text, and speech work. They have a literacy set: "an ability to tune in—with appropriate action—to literacy, with the skills and attitudes necessary for success" (Holdaway 1979, 49).

Some children who have had early exposure and experience with language and books may be resistant to activities associated with reading and writing. Their prior experiences have influenced their attitudes to literacy learning. Some children lack a well-developed literacy set yet have positive attitude toward literacy. For a variety of reasons they have probably experienced few opportunities with books, pencils, and being listened to.

Teachers can confuse the impact of prior literacy experiences with latent ability (Allington 2000), and mistakenly believe that a child's lack of early literacy experiences means a lack of potential to learn. Often children's inability to express themselves and their lack of language experiences makes it difficult to uncover what they already know; thus their potential is not released.

Kindergarten teachers should begin with a fundamental premise: All five year olds coming to school have the ability to learn but they will learn in different ways at different rates. Clay notes that learning occurs on many different physical and mental fronts (1998). All children coming to school have the potential for learning success; it is the teacher's job to determine how to unlock that potential.

Teachers can identify children who have a well-developed literacy set and the attitudes and experiences they have as listeners, viewers, speakers, readers, and writers. In this way, teachers can determine what proficiency looks like at the five-year-old level. This knowledge provides a framework for decisions about individual students: how to shift the attitudes of children who are resistant to reading and writing, and how to bridge the gaps of those who lack certain experiences.

ACQUIRING LANGUAGE

Developing the Listener

Listening means being attentive and responsive. In a home where literacy activities are encouraged, children become part of the family conversation. An infant babbling at the dinner table is beginning to understand that listening and talking is part of family culture.

As speech develops, the responsive adult is asking, "Do you hear that sound? That's a train coming. If we stand here, we'll see it." These opportunities to listen and respond are opportunities to acquire new vocabulary. "You're pointing to the sky. Oh, you can hear those ducks flying over the park. Listen to them—'Quack, quack, quack.' That's a mallard, look at all his colors."

Children's questions about their world are answered because people listen to them. Their willingness to ask questions is encouraged by the adults around them. "How do birds stay up in the air? Why do some daddies have beards and other daddies don't? Why can't a chicken swim? What happens if a pirate injures his other eye?"

They come to school with a million questions.

Young children learn the social conventions of listening from early experiences. They understand that asking questions requires listening for answers. They understand that in some places they have to listen before they can talk. "Please wait until I'm finished talking with your brother. Then I'll listen to you." In a family in which everyone talks at once, children develop different listening and speaking behaviors from other families in which listening and talking mean taking turns.

The developing listener shows evidence of learning behaviors that have occurred as a result of his or her own experiences. Children who enter school knowing that through listening they can learn are at an advantage. Figure 1.1 sets out

What does the young listener do?	What makes it happen?
• Listens attentively • Listens to what others have to say • Listens and responds to others • Listens and responds to books • Asks questions • Interprets information • Asks for clarification • Solves problems by listening • Follows simple directions	• Child listens to stories, conversations, radio, television, audio tapes, video tapes, sounds of the environment • Adults ask questions about what the child is hearing • Adults demonstrate active listening by responding to what has been read or said • Adults listen to and value the child's thinking (the providing of feedback through listening has been instantaneous) • Child asks questions and listens to the answers • Child is part of an audience • Child takes turns in talking and listening to another child or an adult • Adult demonstrates how to listen

Figure 1.1: Developing the Listener

the characteristics of a developing listener and those experiences that increase listening skills. The first column provides list of behaviors that suggest what the developing listener can do. When watching a child in the classroom, where do teachers see evidence of the ability to listen attentively? It's there when the child comments, asks questions, and interprets information.

The second column in Figure 1.1 supports the planning for these learning opportunities. For example, children who lack listening experiences need more opportunities to listen time after time to books on tape. These experiences are supported by helping them think about what to listen for. The chart in Figure 1.1 helps the identification of desired listening behaviors and the experiences needed to develop them.

Developing the Viewer

Viewing is when children create meaning from what they observe. Children are surrounded by visual media. Movies, advertising, television, and the Internet are part of their daily lives. They are informed, entertained, and sometimes frightened by the combination of words and images. It's often hard to make sense of them. "I don't like it when that lady comes on. She has a scary face and makes scary noises with her mouth."

Children hear Mom remark as she looks at the newspaper, "Have you seen the ad for towels? The TV said the sale starts at 8 am tomorrow morning." They also respond to visual media. We hear them say, "I want this truck right here (child points at the Sunday newspaper advertisement). I have a dump truck but I need a cement mixer!"

Children connect their own lives to what they observe. Their growing knowledge of story is developed by viewing their environment and what they see through media. What they see, they play. "Pretend I am the mommy and you are the baby and I am going to feed you dinner. And you are saying, 'Mommy, I want my dinner!'" The supportive adult extends these experiences by participating in them, but also encourages independence by providing opportunities for the child to play with others or alone.

Children also find information through viewing. "You were asking me what Mars would look like if you were up close. Let's see if the Internet has close-up pictures of Mars."

Figure 1.2 sets out the support for the teacher to observe the child's development as a viewer. Teachers watch a child's reaction to different media. They listen to the responses to video, magazines, or the computer. They listen to the child's comments

What does the young viewer do?	What makes it happen?
• Responds to visual media (television, videos, cartoons, advertisements, Internet)	• Child is exposed to a variety of visual media
• Uses visual aids to understand story (dialogue, facial expression, action, and the music that accompanies)	• Adult talks about what is viewed • Child hears questions about what is viewed
• Interprets character through facial expressions, body language, gestures, clothing, actions	• Child hears opinions about what has been viewed
• Identifies qualities that appeal (color, sound, action, scary parts)	• Child sees demonstrations of discussion about visual media
• Differentiates real life from visual media	• Adult listens to child talk about what is being viewed
• Predicts content and meaning based on knowledge and structure of visual media (lengths of video, cartoon, genre)	
• Poses questions while viewing	
• Enjoys talking about what has been viewed	
• Discusses and interprets what has been seen	

Figure 1.2: Developing the Viewer

for opinions or interpretations of what he or she has seen. Encouraging story telling and setting aside time to watch and record students' responses as they participate with or observe others are important aspects of viewing.

Developing the Reader

Children who come to school having many experiences with books are more likely to become high-progress readers. They enjoy listening to a good story. They love returning to favorite books. They delight in the rhyme and rhythm of language.

When reading to children adults stop naturally to look at the pictures... "This looks just like Sali's dog, don't you think?"... to explore rich language... "And he huffed and he puffed and he blew the house down!"... to provide opportunities for anticipation... "Uh-oh, look at his face. I think something bad is going to happen."... to pose questions wondering about what will happen next... "There's that frog again, I wonder what trouble he'll get into this time." These are all components of what readers do when they read. By listening, the child has become part of the process of reading, part of the closeness and intimacy of reading with another.

In a rich, literate environment, books are available in the home for the children to return to over and over. The child has time to play at reading. The child retells the story that has been heard over and over, "And Cinderella said—you are not a nice lady stepmother! I don't like you one bit!" They have regular experiences holding the book, knowing where to start and how to turn the pages, and knowing what to do with the book when they are finished reading. "They lived happily ever after and that's the end!"

Opportunities to observe what readers do when they read, the interactions with the adult reader, and spending time with books independently all contribute toward the child's literacy set.

Figure 1.3 indicates what teachers look for in developing readers when they are handed a book. Teachers are looking for the child who is playing at reading, using the pictures and his or her own conversation to tell the story. Teachers listen for what the child knows about story, not only when he or she holds a book but also when it's read to them. Teachers watch students' interactions with puppets, dress-ups, and flannel board stories to see if they have a repertoire of

---

THE DEVELOPING READER

Phoebe crawls into bed with Granddad and Granny Jan each morning when she visits. She comes with her favorite book in hand, the one that has to do with a queen and jelly beans. This book doesn't have much appeal to Granddad, so he makes up a new story each time he reads.

One morning when Phoebe is about four and a half, and Granddad has left the room, she turns seriously to her grandmother and says, "Granny Jan, we have a problem. Granddad can't read."

Granny Jan looks at her and replies, "Well then, Phoebe, I guess you'll have to learn how to so we can teach him."

What does the young reader do?	What makes it happen?
• Enjoys books	• Child is read to from infancy
• Anticipates while being read to	• Child talks about books as they are read
• Chooses to look at books	• Child hears poems, jingles, songs, word-play, nursery rhymes
• Knows where to start to read	
• Knows front and back	• Child is familiar with books, poems, jingles, songs because they have been repeated over and over again
• Knows pictures as a source of information	
	• Child joins in repetitive sessions
• Uses pictures to retell story	• Child anticipates through a pausing in the voice of the reader
• Uses book language in retelling	
• Expects print to remain constant	• Child enjoys shared experiences with books that are pleasurable and interactive
• Identifies some punctuation	
• Seeks book experiences	• Child has access to books and returns to them independently
• Shows interest in print	• Child reads and rereads books
• Creates images/drawings based on stories	• Child talks about book features (title, illustrations, author)
• Uses sounds and intonation to tell stories	• Child recognizes and talks about print features (letters, words, spaces, punctuation)
• Understands how stories work	
• Recognizes familiar print in his or her environment	

Figure 1.3: Developing the Reader

familiar stories, to see if book language appears in their retellings, and to listen for intonation that reveals the subtleties of the story. Teachers pay attention to the natural curiosity the child has about print and listen for the child's awareness of sounds in language. They want to hear rhyme and rhythm become part of the child's conversation.

Teachers select books for the classroom library that they know will invite children to read and reread. They make certain that children with limited book experiences are read to many times daily. They are interested in the quality of the stories children hear and in the number they read.

When reading to children, teachers talk aloud about how the text is making them feel and what it causes them to wonder. They also expose children to the rhyme and rhythm of language through poetry and songs.

PRODUCING LANGUAGE

Developing the Speaker

When children first begin to talk, adults respond to their attempts in positive ways. "Did you hear that?? I think he said Dad!" Such a natural response from adults provides support for learning. Adults repeating what the child is trying to say also provides a demonstration of how the word is supposed to sound. "Juush?" "Oh, you'd like some juice? Do you want apple or orange juice?"

A child immersed in talk all day and every day begins to understand how language works. He or she understands different intonations mean different things.

THE DEVELOPING SPEAKER

Each day, Chad is someone else.

On Monday he is the firefighter.

He places the microphone against his mouth and begins. "We've got a fire on that street over there. I need the tall ladder engine sent right now!"

On Tuesday, he is a motorcycle police officer.

"Emergency, emergency. Put out the APB. We're following a black sedan, license plate 27E."

On Wednesday, he is an astronaut.

"I need to get my space suit on now. We are ready to blast off!"

On Thursday, he is a doctor.

"You have a broken leg. I will cover you with a plaster cast and that will make it better. Don't forget to use those sticks (pointing to crutches) or you will fall down!"

"Get off that sofa, Fluffy! You know you're not allowed up there." From daily examples the child becomes a talker, asking questions, "How many more miles till we get there?" They negotiate. "I would like another drink and another story, please." They demand. "I want that toy right now!"

Stories encourage vocabulary development. Whether stories are told or read, children are able to question and clarify meaning. "What is a troll?" "Which one is the salamander?" Through repetition, book language begins to creep into conversation. "I want that chair because it's 'just right'!" Developing oral language is part of developing a literacy set.

Figure 1.4 characterizes the young speaker. Teachers listen for their descriptions of experiences, their questions, and how they ask for clarifications. They observe their expressive language in their group interactions. Are they able to negotiate and discuss? What is their level of vocabulary development?

What does the young speaker do?	What makes it happen?
• Talks about self and his or her experiences	• Child develops oral language because of demonstrations from significant others
• Tells a story	• Child sees and participates in social conversation
• Recites something they know	
• Describes	• Child sees and participates in intimate conversations
• Uses book language along with natural language when he or she talks	• Child sees demonstrations of discussion
• Expresses him- or herself to a group	• Child listens to a variety of adult conversations
• Negotiates meanings and uncovers confusions	• Child is given time to talk in order to receive a response
• Presents information	• Child is continually interacting with more competent speakers
• Poses questions	
• Discusses what has been read	• Child experiences the need to listen and talk in order for conversation to happen
• Talks about own writing	• Child sees pleasure in using new words
• Interprets verbally	
• Expresses self easily and often	

Figure 1.4: Developing the Speaker

Teachers are aware of the need for continued language development for children, so they know the kindergarten classroom will not be a quiet place. They expect that as children interact in the library, as they write, or as they engage in any learning around the room, the learning will be supported by talk. In any classroom talk is bound by social norms. There is time for talking and time for being quiet. This too must be learned.

In providing time for individual children to talk, teachers must be good listeners, knowing when and how to respond. Children's language increases through a teacher's demonstrations, discussions, what has been read to them, and by careful listening.

Developing the Presenter

Children can interpret their world by presenting. They recreate events in their lives through play. Children use materials around them to communicate their messages. A stick might be the magician's wand or the soup spoon. Voices and facial expressions convey meaning as they dramatize the latest story, an experience or a television program. Drawings provide another way of communicating what may not be as easy to say. Simple words and signs can say it all. "How do

What does the young presenter do?	What makes it happen?
• Imitates visual media (television, videos, cartoons, advertisements, Internet)	• Child is exposed to a variety of visual media
• Dramatizes character through use of facial expressions, body language, gestures, clothing, actions	• Child has access to materials for storytelling (puppets, dress-ups, flannel board figures)
• Uses visual aids to present story (music, dialogue, facial expression, action)	• Child plays and dramatizes what has been seen
• Presents information through storytelling	• Child receives adult response to dramatization
• Controls content and meaning through storytelling	• Child is provided opportunity to draw pictures
• Represents information visually through drawing and illustration	• Child receives adult response to sketches and illustrations
• Develops clarity and fluency in letter formation	

Figure 1.5: Developing the Presenter

THE DEVELOPING PRESENTER

Simon was with his father. They had run a few errands and then stopped by his father's friend Mark's house for a quick visit. Simon's father remarked that they needed to be quick because it was nearly Simon's bedtime.

Simon engaged Mark in acting out a story. He told Mark who all of the characters were. Simon was the boy and Mark was the dad.

The story was about a boy who had come home from school, only to find that his father was not home and he had no key. The boy immediately used his cell phone, relating an elaborate description of the problem, with voice and facial expressions that left no one to wonder how he felt.

The "father" in the story gave a reasonable response, telling the "boy" where he could find the key. The boy looked in the imaginary spot, only to report (once again, via the cell phone) that no key was to be found.

"Father" (sensing that it was time for Simon and his Dad to go home to put Simon to bed) came up with another logical solution—another key could be found at the neighbors. Simon rejected that solution as well and the story continued.

With each solution, Simon introduced a new problem. Mark was stymied.

Simon's father ended the story when he scooped him up and took him home to bed.

you write, 'All Girls Keep Out?'", John asks his Dad after a little argument with his sisters. He has the paper, markers, and masking tape ready to make a sign for his door.

In order to observe the behaviors of these developing presenters teachers create classroom spaces for children to present daily. There are boxes of puppets, a flannel board and characters, and boxes filled with costumes. There is an area of the classroom for drawing and illustration with papers of different sizes and paints and markers of all colors. Teachers watch for the behaviors set out in Figure 1.5.

Developing the Writer

Children who enter school with a well-defined literacy set view writing as something people do to communicate with each other. They have had the opportunity to see writers writing (Woodward, Harste, and Burke 1984). Adult writers provide natural demonstrations about what writers do and—as they talk aloud—how writers think. Children hear what is going on in the writer's head as the writer writes.

THE DEVELOPING WRITER

Hannah's mom is away on a business trip, and after her return, Hannah writes this story.

Mom stepped off a plane.

Mom brings home presents.

She gives her kid a hug and kiss and they lived happily ever after.

"I can't forget to tell grandma that we'll be down for the holidays. That will make her really happy!"

"Make sure I write *peanut butter* down on the grocery list so you can have a sandwich tomorrow."

Children know writers use pens, paper, and keyboards. They can talk about what their writing says. A child writes a prescription after a visit to the pediatrician and explains it.

"This tells you that you need to take a pill and if you don't take a pill you need to go back to the doctor because you're sick."

What does the young writer do?	What makes it happen?
• Wants to write	• Child sees other people write
• Writes stories	• Child is interested in what the writer is demonstrating
• Knows what is said can be written down	• Child has pencils and paper available
• Knows print holds meaning	• Child is interested in knowing more
• Uses own experiences to compose a message	• Child is motivated to try
• Draws pictures and scribbles to generate and express ideas	• Child is encouraged to take a risk
• Talks about pictures	• Child's approximations are valued
• Knows where to start writing	• Child's talk about letters, sounds, words is naturally present
• Writes left to right, top to bottom across a page	• Child's writing is given to a reader
• Understands why people write	• Child sees a purpose for writing
• Distinguishes one letter from another	
• Constructs words from letters	
• Approximates letters, sounds, and words when writing	

Figure 1.6: Developing the Writer

Adults talk about letters, words, and sounds in their writing. The child listens, makes comments and asks questions, "Look!" (Sam points to an *s*) "This one is like my name." "That big one is like 'mommy,' " a four year old reports when looking at an *m* in a magazine title.

Children approximate as writers. Adults who respond in positive ways to approximations support the learning of the developing writer.

Figure 1.6 characterizes the behaviors of young writers. To observe writing behaviors, children must have opportunities to write every day. Teachers observe how their drawings and conversation support the ideas children have for writing. Observation provides information about their current understanding of directionality, letters, and sounds.

LANGUAGE MODES AND THE LITERACY SET

Understanding the behaviors that comprise a literacy set enables teachers to:

- Know what to look for when gathering information about incoming kindergarten students.
- Know the foundational skills for the development of listeners/speakers, readers/writers, viewers, and presenters.
- Know the environment that should be provided in the classroom for learning to occur.
- Know the learning that needs to occur.

A literacy set provides a solid foundation for learning, a foundation for success in literacy. Students who come to school without a well-developed literacy set need support to extend their learning. Teachers recognize that some children have strengths in one mode over another. They provide experiences in ways that children learn and that supports them meeting the community's expectations and standards as listeners, speakers, readers, writers, viewers, and presenters.

Chapter 2 explores the tools teachers can use to gather information about where each kindergarten student is along the developmental continuum of literacy learning.

2 knowing the learners upon entry to kindergarten

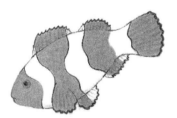

Chapter 1 focused on the importance of learning about what constitutes a literacy set. Teachers need tools to assess the quality of the literacy experiences children have had prior to school entry. They need to know something of the child's home and cultural background; this allows them to "build a bridge between home and school literacies" (Neuman 2001, 260). All children have had language experiences. Teachers should learn the extent to which these experiences have formed their attitudes and understandings about literacy.

Typically, children from a mainstream, middle-class culture have opportunities prior to school that replicate what they will do in school. Parents read books to children and use the same story language that teachers use. They engage children in school-like questioning where children are asked questions and adults already know the answer (Panofsky 1994). It can be different for children from other cultures. Studies of African American families (Heath 1983; Vernon-Feagans 1996) describe children's preschool literacy experiences where texts were read aloud in a group setting. Group members made meaning together as they embellished a written text through story telling. African American children typically lacked books in the home but were expected to tell stories about real events. Often these stories involved contributions from children of different ages. While these experiences might be different from those of other children they were also rich and meaningful, but not necessarily supportive of school expectations.

Knowing the literacy experiences and cultural background of each child enables a teacher to be sensitive to how these differences can impact the child's success in school. The task is not to underestimate the importance of each child's heritage, but rather to recognize their experiences as different not deficient, and acknowledge the impact of a child's experiences upon how school works.

MY CLASS

My class is a real class of children. I have watched their progress through a whole year of teaching and learning. For the purpose of the narrative, I request the reader's indulgence to allow me, in the first person, to journey as their teacher through a year in kindergarten.

- There are 23 children in this class.
- There are 11 girls and 12 boys.
- Their ethnicity consists of White, Hispanic, Native American, and African American.
- They speak English, Spanish, Navajo, and Serbo-Croatian.
- The English language learners' families are from Mexico and Bosnia.
- The overall socio-economic status of the school is low. Eighty-seven percent of students receive a free or reduced-cost lunch.

I have gathered additional information about these children from talking with their families and observing them during the first few weeks of school. These discussions confirm or challenge my assessment about the children's literacy development. I can also decide how to support families, smoothing their child's transition from home to kindergarten.

HALF-DAY VS. FULL-DAY KINDERGARTEN

The classroom in this book is a full-day kindergarten but the intent and expectations would not differ if it was a program for children attending half-day. All kindergarten classrooms must be very intentional in the use of time. Because less time is available in the half-day, every minute must count. Teachers must consider carefully how time is used.

ASSESSING ATTITUDES TOWARD LEARNING

Children enter kindergarten with a range of attitudes about literacy and school. Some children have confidence in their ability to read and write despite their literacy experiences. Others with more developed literacy behaviors lack confidence and take few risks. There are a few who resist anything that has to do with books, pencils, and paper. I have some children with limited experiences of being in a group or listening carefully for directions. Their attitudes and behaviors indicate the potential for independence and taking personal responsibility.

There are questions I ask myself as I observe children engaged in literacy activities during the first few weeks of school.

- Has the child had preschool experiences, listened to stories, participated in whole and small group activities?
- Can the child listen to others, understand what it means to get in line, wait for a turn, follow directions or ask for help?
- Does the child appear confident?
- How does the child handle frustrations and deal with others?
- How does the child make decisions?
- What are the child's special interests?

The assessment data gathered becomes the first part of a literacy portrait. It helps me begin to reach important decisions about learning needs.

ASSESSING STRENGTHS

Teachers can decide to assess literacy skills in two ways. The first concerns what children are not able to do. The second concerns what they can do. Figure 2.1 illustrates how these two perspectives provide different starting points for learning. It is a writing sample of an emergent writer in kindergarten. From the first perspective, it could be argued that scribbles are not writing, and that the child would have to learn letters and sounds before he is able to communicate meaning. Notes the teacher might make concerning this writing sample could include the following:

- Unable to write (scribbles)
- Knows no letters or sounds.

From the second perspective, it could be concluded that the writer knows that writing carries meaning because he has drawn a sketch of two people above the writing. This was confirmed when the child was asked what he had written. He replied that the story was about his sister; that she is a cheerleader at high school, that she has pom-poms, and when she jumps in the air the pom-poms fling all over. It was obvious the writer began on the left side of the page and worked to the right with a return sweep. He also began at the top of the page and worked toward the bottom. Also there are attempts to use the letters in his name in the writing. Notes about this writer could include the following:

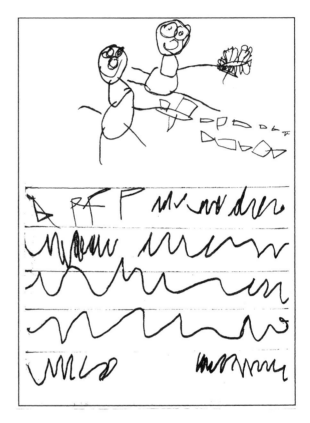

Figure 2.1: A Writing Sample

- Understands writing makes meaning.
- Sketches to convey meaning.
- Has left to right and return sweep in own writing.
- Uses initial letter of name in writing.

Why would two observations of the same child and the same piece of writing provide such different information? In the first case the child is seen with a deficit. In the second case a teacher has looked for evidence of what the child *can* do. The teacher's task is to take each child on to the next step along a literacy continuum by building upon those strengths.

The challenge of working from deficits is that they are always there. On the other hand, working from strengths means there is always a new foundation to build upon. Assessment data shows where the child is on the learning continuum through the literacy strengths already gained (Crooks 1988).

To discover these strengths in early literacy development, teachers can observe students as they engage in authentic literacy tasks. They can use a number of assessment tools. In the rest of this chapter we explore two tools used to assess student literacy behavior: *My Book* (Duncan 2005) and *An Observation Survey of Early Literacy Achievement* (Clay 2002).

TOOLS FOR ASSESSING LITERACY BEHAVIORS

My Book

My Book (Duncan 2005) has been designed as an informal assessment tool to provide relevant data about the literacy attitudes, knowledge, and skills of students entering kindergarten. Directions for administering this assessment can be found in Appendix A. A wide range of skills can be assessed through its use. Teachers can determine the particular information they wish to gather.

For teachers new to observational assessment, this tool provides a friendly starting point toward knowing the kinds of relevant data that can inform their instruction. For teachers more experienced in gathering assessment data, this simple tool introduces children to working in small groups and provides a useful source of additional data about literacy acquisition.

My Book can be administered in a variety of ways. Certain items might be presented to the whole group. For instance, one item asks children to draw a self-portrait and write their names (Figure 2.2). A teacher can give instructions to the children in whole group, then move about the room monitoring and encouraging children as they draw and write.

Figure 2.2: Page 2 of *My Book*

Some items can be administered in small groups. This serves two purposes. First, it provides the teacher an opportunity to observe individual literacy behaviors more closely. One item invites children to talk about what they do at home ("At home I like to _____."). The teacher can observe how the child can relate his or her experiences. There is an opportunity with this item to observe each child's movement left to right, and how each child records sounds he or she hears, writes words he or she knows, and illustrates ideas.

Administration in small groups also gives a teacher a chance to introduce children to small group work. As they participate in the group, they learn the expectations for group work. Other children in the class also become familiar with the expectation of what to do when the teacher is instructing a small group. When a group is working with the teacher, for example, the rest of the class might be working on a project or activity they can complete without the teacher's help. This is especially important at the beginning of the year.

Figure 2.3: Page 10 of *My Book*

A few items may lend themselves to individual administration, especially where additional support is required or where the teacher wishes to gather specific information. In others, the teacher may use this one-on-one time for an extended conversation with the child. The final page of the assessment asks the child to identify a favorite book. This topic prompted an interesting exchange with one child who said, "He was a big crow and he talks. He was half-human and half-bird. It was a scary book." The child was not able to provide the title, but he revealed a rather sophisticated description of the character. This rich description may not have been revealed in a small or whole group situation.

My favorite book is CAT IN THE HAT

12

Figure 2.4: Page 12 of *My Book*

Appendix A provides questions about a child's developing skills and attitudes toward literacy that the teacher can ask. The back cover of *My Book* includes a note to the parents or caregivers (Figure 2.5) explaining the purpose of the book, how the child was supported in completing it, and what the teacher is expecting to learn from the child's responses.

The benefits to the teacher using *My Book* as an assessment tool not only include the assessment data that is gathered, but also develops children's expectations about working together as a whole group, being part of a small group, and taking responsibility as an individual. This experience provides the beginnings of forming good work habits, classroom routines, and understanding what it means to function independently in a classroom with others. Also, the strengths of the incoming kindergarten students are available to parents, as well as communicating the message that literacy learning will occur in kindergarten. Finally, *My Book* is meaningful to children because it provides a text that can be read and reread.

Dear Parents,
The beginning of school is an exciting time for your child and an exciting time for me! We have begun the journey of kindergarten.

This special book, *My Book*, is designed especially to record what your child can do as we begin kindergarten.

It also provides me valuable information about your child's literacy strengths. From these pages, I can determine how your child:
■ Handles books, turns pages,
■ Talks about the pictures and talks about experiences,
■ Follows the words on the page, one by one,
■ Records sounds with corresponding letters,
■ Holds a pencil; forms letters,
■ Writes his or her name,
■ Draws pictures,
■ And a lot more!

It's not important that your child currently knows all these skills, but it is important that I know what your child can do. Knowing what your child already knows helps me decide exactly what to teach next.

When reading this book with your child, it is important to focus on the content of the book. At this time, I would not expect your child to spell all of the words correctly or "get everything right." I am happy with what they have attempted.

I encourage you to save this little book. Bring it along to our first parent/teacher conference so we can look at where your child's journey began and how much learning has occurred.

Sincerely,
Your child's teacher

Figure 2.5:
Back Cover of
My Book

An Observation Survey of Early Literacy Achievement

An Observation Survey of Early Literacy Achievement (Clay 2002) is a collection of more formal assessment tools that provide valuable information regarding the development of a child's literacy set. Data derived from the survey can be used to assess where the child is along the literacy learning continuum and what the child already knows. The data can also point toward the child's next step for learning and, for the experienced teacher, what has to be planned for as instruction.

The Observation Survey is standardized by procedures used to administer the six tasks in the survey. It is a systematic and sensitive assessment of early literacy behaviors. Stanines (see Clay 2002, 55) provide valuable comparative data about the individual child, the class as a whole, or across a grade level for specific age groups of students. *The Observation Survey of Early Literacy Achievement* is administered to each child individually, adhering to specific guidelines. Teachers may be fortunate enough to bring children into the classroom individually prior to school opening. Alternatively they may be released for a few hours each week after the first few weeks of school to collect this information. Usually the Observation Survey is administered in the first few weeks of school. Regardless of how time is allocated, the important part of the administration is finding sufficient time to be with each individual child. Time alone with the child is the opportunity to gather assessment data and develop a relationship.

The more familiar the teacher is with administrating the survey, the easier it is to evaluate the quality of literacy behaviors as each child works through the tasks. Teachers should be interested in the child's attitude toward learning. While remaining a neutral observer, the teacher's goal is to provide children the opportunity to realize their potential. The survey allows time to show what they are capable of doing. Because this tool is administered in a one-on-one situation, encouragement fosters pride in accomplishments. The teacher has this opportunity to allow the child to show what he or she can do.

Letter identification task

In the letter identification task, the child is asked to identify all upper- and lowercase letters as they would be handwritten or found in print text. There are a total of 54 symbols tested. A letter is scored as correct if the child has identified it by name, a sound, or a word beginning.

The teacher asks,

- What can the child do?
  - What letters does the child know?
  - What was the level of confidence in which the child completed the task?
- What is the child attempting to do?
  - What letters has the child confused (e.g., *b/d*)?
- What does the child need to learn next?
  - What letters need to be known?

A CLOSER LOOK THROUGH CASE STUDIES

In the pages that follow, the literacy experiences of my incoming kindergarten class are collected and analyzed. The data represents a range of students with diverse needs. It's typical of most kindergarten classrooms. As case studies of the progress that typical children in my class will make through the year, I have selected three children with differing prior knowledge experiences to examine closely: one child with a limited literacy set, one child with some literacy experiences, and one child with a well-developed literacy set. We will meet these students again throughout the book.

Celia

Celia is a limited English speaker. Her receptive language is growing. She understands much of what is being said to her. She responds in English when talking with her friends and me. I hear her use English on the playground. Right now the playground is her favorite place, and she makes it known what she wants to do. Celia lacks the prior experiences that would have prepared her for school, so adjusting to the norms of school has been a challenge. Initially, she spent much of the school day under the table and would protest loudly when asked to come out. After two weeks of school, she is willing to participate in what we do, if only as an observer.

Julio

Julio exudes confidence. Spanish is the primary language spoken at home, but Julio is proficient in both English and Spanish. He is outgoing and enthusiastic about his learning. He has a lot to say about everything we are doing in kindergarten and is thoroughly enjoying the experiences. He is attentive and quick to bring his background knowledge to stories he hears. He has been willing to try most anything.

Nina

Nina is a Navajo child who is quiet and reserved, and she has been initially hesitant to take a risk. She frequently asks, "Is this right?" She said very little the first few weeks of school. Her demeanor initially caused me to think she was a passive learner until I saw her pick up a book in the book area and begin to read it. I believe she is an astute observer of her surroundings and that under the surface this quiet child is someone who may know more than is obvious.

TASK 1: LETTER IDENTIFICATION

Celia's Letter Identification

Celia has little alphabet knowledge but a natural curiosity. Within the first two weeks of school, she has developed an interest in learning. She smiles as she identifies the letters. She can identify the letter C and is aware that this is the first letter in her name. She uses other letter names through the list, although incorrectly. Celia needs to learn both upper and lower case letters. My initial notes say:

Letter Identification

- 1/54 (Stanine 1)
- Willingly attempts task
- Willingness to take risks; perseveres
- Knows letter name c
- Next step—letters in name.

Julio's Letter Identification

Julio correctly identified 43 of 54 letters in the letter identification task. He knows all uppercase letters. Julio confused the letters b/d, h/n, m/w, q/b, r/f, and did not know lowercase h, n, q, r, g, and l. He confused the letter l with the number 1. He quickly named letters, stopping every now and again to comment on how well he was at doing this task. My notes say:

Letter Identification

- 43/54 (Stanine 5)
- High level of confidence
- Knows all uppercase letters
- Confusions $\frac{b\ h\ m\ q\ r}{d\ n\ w\ b\ f}$
- Confused letter l with number 1
- Next step—clear up confusions (d, n, w, b, f), learn h, n, q, r, g, l.

Nina's Letter Identification

At the beginning of the assessment, Nina was asked, "What are these?" I pointed to the letters. She quickly responded, "Letters," with a quizzical look on her face, as if she was wondering that I really didn't know! Nina identified 52 of 54 letters. Her confusions were with the letter l, which she named I, and q, which after hesitating, she named o. My notes read:

Letter Identification

- 52/54 (Stanine 6)
- Knows all uppercase and most lowercase
- Confusion $\dfrac{I\ o}{l\ q}$
- Next step—letters l, q.

The Observation Survey scores can be reported in raw scores and in stanines. Raw scores are simply the number of items in the task when the child has scored correctly. "Stanines are scores which redistribute raw scores according to a normal curve in nine groups from 1 (a low score) to 9 (a high score)" (Clay 2002, 121). Stanines allow the teacher to compare each student's scores across all tasks.

Figure 2.6 represents the results from the Letter Identification task for my class. It compares raw scores with stanines as illustrated. The stanines are derived from a random sample of children ages 5.0 to 5.5 in New Zealand in the year 2000.

LETTER IDENTIFICATION

Beginning of Year Results

Stanine	1	2	3	4	5	6	7	8	9
Raw Score Range	0–3	4–12	13–27	28–42	43–49	50–52	53	54	54
# of Students	7	3	3	4	2	3	0	I	
% of Students	30.43	13.04	13.04	17.4	8.69	13.04		4.34	

Figure 2.6: Class Data for Letter Identification

The data tells me there is a significant difference in the experiences these children have had with the alphabet. Ten children know 28 letters or more, three children know fourteen letters, and ten children know between zero and four letters. Teaching a letter a week to the whole class will not work. Some of the children know most of the alphabet letters. Half of the children will need to make more progress than one letter per week.

TASK 2: CONCEPTS ABOUT PRINT

The Concepts about Print (CAP) task uncovers what children understand about written language. When administering the task, I learn what children know about how text and print works.

Clay states, "It is easy to observe what children already know by using the Concepts About Print observation task, and the teacher will be better prepared to advance any child's understanding when they already know what children are attending to" (2002, 37). Individual concepts receive points totaling 24.

The questions I ask myself when looking at individuals are as follows:

- What are the student's strengths in knowing how print works? Can the student identify the front of the book, directionality, the fact that print carries a message, letters and letter clusters, words, the concepts of first and last, upper- and lowercase letters, and punctuation?
- What is the student attempting to do?
- What does the student need to learn next?

Celia's Concepts about Print

Celia enjoys this task and doesn't hesitate to respond when I ask her questions. Her responses are not oral. Celia points with her finger. She identifies the bottom of a page. Her score in this subtest was 1 out of 24. This confirms what the letter identification task showed me: her limited English. It appears she has limited experiences with print and books in English. It may also be apparent that she does not yet understand the language of what was being asked of her. I note her responses as follows:

Concepts about Print

- 1/24 (Stanine 1)
- Identifies bottom of page
- Next step—front and back of book.

Julio's Concepts about Print

Julio exhibits confidence in the Concept about Print task. He identifies the front of the book and points to the print when asked where to start reading. He points out that a left page needs to be read before the right. While he understands print goes from left to right, he does not yet control the skill of return sweep. He knows "first and last" and recognizes when the print is upside down. When being asked what a period is for, Julio replies that it is "a stop." He identifies the concept of a letter by differentiating between one letter and two letters. His score was 9 of a possible 24. I note Julio's responses as follows:

Concepts about Print

- Knows front of book, where to begin, L to R, left page before right
- Print contains a message, recognizes inverted print, meaning of period
- Letter concept (one letter, two letters)
- Next step—return sweep.

Nina's Concepts about Print

Nina is experienced with books and print. She reads aloud as I read. Her book handling skills are automatic; she knows where to begin and how text works. She is aware of changes in the order of letters ("It's not right writing."). She identifies a period ("It means to stop"), a question mark ("It's asking someone a question"), and a comma ("It means to pause"). She isolates letters and identifies capital letters. Though confusions arise with the concepts of "first and last" (first and last part of story, line order, left page before right, and first and last letter). Nina's score is 18 of 24 points. I note her responses as follows:

Concepts about Print

- Has book orientation, directionality, word-by-word matching, inverted print, change in letter order, punctuation (. , ?) upper- and lowercase letters, difference between a letter and word, word order (*was, no*)
- Approximations—first and last confusions (part of story, page, line order, word order, first and last word)
- Next step—first and last.

Figure 2.7 shows that most of the students in the classroom are able to find the front of the book and have some knowledge about directionality. Two children (stanines 7 and 8) show significant experiences with the way text works. This data confirms the range of experiences of learning in this classroom.

CONCEPTS ABOUT PRINT

Beginning of Year Results

Stanine	1	2	3	4	5	6	7	8	9
Raw Score Range	0–7	8–9	10–11	12–13	14	15–16	17–18	19	20+
# of Students	13	3	1	2	0	0	1	1	0
% of Students	56.5	13	4.3	8.7	0	0	4.3	4.3	0

Figure 2.7: Class Data for Concepts about Print

TASK 3: WRITING VOCABULARY

In the Writing Vocabulary task, I observe children writing words they know. I encourage children to start with their name. The guidelines permit me to suggest words the child might know and to offer a prompt when needed (words like *I, a, is, Mom, Dad*). The task is to be completed in ten minutes. At this point in the year, some children do not require the maximum time. All are encouraged to continue writing. One point is scored for each word spelled correctly.

I ask myself these questions about the children's responses:

- What does the child know about his or her name?
- What does the child know about letters and words?
- What additional information can I gather such as left to right sequencing, pencil grip, formation of letters, orientation of writing to the page?
- What is the child approximating?
- What is the optimal next step for each writer?

Celia's Writing Vocabulary

Celia is excited to select a colored marker for her writing. She talks about purple being her favorite color. I tell her I want to see how many words she can write, and I ask if she can write her name. She says yes, and immediately begins to write (Figure 2.8).

Figure 2.8: Celia's Writing

Celia shows familiarity with several letters in her name. She reverses *c*, writes another *c* accurately, and immediately writes another larger *c* on top of that. She points to the larger *c* and says, "It is big!" This could show an indication that she has some sense of the need for a capital letter as the first letter. She continues by writing an *e* and an *l* and another *e*. She uses lowercase letters for the *e* and *l*. She is able to write three of five letters in her name. We talk about writing more words, but Celia stops after her name. I note her responses to this task:

Writing Vocabulary

- 0 (Stanine 1)
- Can write three letters in her name *C-e-l*
- Writes lowercase *e* and *l*
- Approximates understanding that first name begins with capital letter
- Next step—writing name.

Julio's Writing Vocabulary

Julio loses confidence when asked to write. He shows a reluctance that is not evident when he is asked to interact with books. He says, "I can't write my name. I can't write anything!" After a bit of encouragement and some conversation about his name, Julio makes an attempt (Figure 2.9).

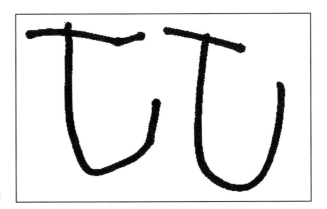

Figure 2.9: Julio's Writing

Although reversed, Julio writes the letters *J-J*. I will check to see if this is a family nickname. I note his responses to this task as follows:

Writing Vocabulary

- 0 (Stanine 1)
- Writes initial letters of name (is this a nickname?) Reverses *J*
- Less confident with writing
- Next step—Writing name.

Nina's Writing Vocabulary

Nina approaches this task with the seriousness of the other tasks. She seems to enjoy our time together (Figure 2.10).

Figure 2.10: Nina's Writing

She writes her name, the names of her sister, her cousin, and a friend. She writes the words *my, me, can, you, love, yes, no,* and *we*. She approximates the word *the*. Her printing is large. She writes in all capital letters except for a lower case *n* in her name. I note her response to the task:

Writing Vocabulary

- Score 12 (Stanine 6)
- Writes own name and names of sister and friends (*Cori, Bety, Brian*)
- Writes high-frequency words (*me, my, can, we, love, you, yes, no*)
- Writes large in upper case except for one letter in name (*n*)
- Next step—lower case letters.

Figure 2.11 sets out the trends for Writing Vocabulary.

WRITING VOCABULARY

Beginning of Year Results

Stanine	1	2	3	4	5	6	7	8	9
Raw Score Range	0	1	2–3	4–6	7–11	12–18	19–32	33–48	49+
# of Students	7	6	5	2	1	2	0	0	0
% of Students	30.43	26.08	21.73	8.69	4.34	8.69	0	0	0

Figure 2.11: Class Data for Writing Vocabulary

These students appear to have had more experiences with the alphabet letters than with words. Three quarters of the students can write their name. This is a good starting point in understanding the concept of a word and making links to other words they can learn.

TASK 4: HEARING AND RECORDING SOUNDS IN WORDS

The administration of this task requires the dictation of a sentence to individual children. They write the letter sounds they hear in the words dictated. Any sound the child records correctly is credited, even though the word may not be spelled conventionally. The task shows evidence of the child's ability to go "from phonemic awareness to letter-sound relationships" (Clay 2002, 120). There are 37 possible sounds and clusters of sounds that can be recorded.

I ask myself about the children's responses:

- What can the child do and what is the child attempting to do?
    - What sounds or clusters of sounds does the child hear?
    - What letters or letter clusters is the child using to represent sounds?
    - What is the evidence of the child's ability to sequence sounds and letters?
    - What is the evidence of some knowledge of words?
    - Does the child see him- or herself as a writer?
    - Is the child willing to approximate; to take risks?
    - What do I learn from the child's approximations?
    - Can the child say the word slowly, even if he or she doesn't match the correct letter to the sound?
- What does the child need to learn next?
    - What would be the optimal next step for the child?

Celia's Hearing and Recording Sounds in Words

Celia is very tentative at the beginning of this task. She selects a marker, listens carefully to the dictated story, then puts her marker very close to the paper but makes no marks. I watch as the marker gets closer and closer and still no mark. After a pause, I suggest she touch the marker to the paper to see if it works. She makes a mark, I praise her efforts, and I dictate the story once again. She takes off! (Figure 2.12)

Celia's writing starts on the left side of the page and goes from left to right in the first line, a skill that was not evident when she was reading. She picks up her marker at the end of each word, poised and ready for the next word. She is making letter-like forms (*m, g, c, s*) and beginning to show confidence as a writer. I note her responses to this task as follows:

Figure 2.12: Celia's Hearing and Recording Sounds in Words

Hearing and Recording Sounds in Words

- 0/37 (Stanine 1)
- Knows where to start, writes from left to right on first line
- Makes letter like forms (*m, g, c, s*)
- Begins to show confidence as a writer
- Return sweep from right to left
- Next step—return sweep.

Julio's Hearing and Recording Sounds in Words

Julio listens to the dictated story (*The bus is coming. It will stop here to let me get on.*) and has a great conversation with me about riding the bus to school, where he waits, and other children who get on at the same stop. The conversation seems to alleviate some of the concerns he showed with the writing vocabulary task. He begins to write (Figure 2.13).

Figure 2.13: Julio's Hearing and Recording Sounds in Words

PHONEMIC AWARENESS

Definition: The ability to hear and identify individual sounds— or phonemes—in spoken words (Armbruster et al. 2001).

What do we need to know?

A child's ability to hear and identify sounds in words is one predictor of reading success. Children who have developed phonemic awareness will also be supported as they record the sounds they hear when writing.

Children who have phonemic awareness are able to recognize:

- Individual sounds in words

- The same sounds in different words

- The word in a set of three or four words that has a different sound.

Phonemic awareness instruction can occur when teachers are reading aloud to students, through the use of poetry, rhymes, and chants, in small group work with alphabet games and oral language development, and as children articulate sounds they hear as they write.

Assessment Tools

The teacher needs to determine a child's phonemic awareness prior to beginning any instruction. The Hearing and Recording Sounds task in *An Observation Survey of Early Literacy Achievement* can provide individual information about the ability of a child to hear sounds in words. Listening and watching children in small groups as they manipulate sounds when using alphabet games and word cards is another way to determine their understanding of phonemic awareness. Commercial assessment tools are also available.

Julio writes the letter *p*. I read the next word in the story. He looks at the bottom of the page, where the word "COMMENT" is written, and begins to carefully copy the word. His attention to the print at the bottom of the paper makes me think he is aware that writing contains letters. When he finishes, he looks at it again and inserts a forgotten letter *N* where it belongs. I continue to read, and a few times, he says, "I don't know that word." Toward the end of the sentence, he draws the large black circle in Figure 2.14 and says, "That's the tire on the bus!

I note his responses to this as follows:

Hearing and Recording Sounds in Words

Figure 2.14: Julio's Drawing Related to the Dictated Story

- 0/37 (Stanine 1)
- Writes from left to right
- Understands writing contains letters
- Understands that words contain letters in a sequence (locates missing letter and replaces in correct place)
- Links pictures to meaning (drawing of a tire)
- Next step—gain confidence in writing.

Nina's Hearing and Recording Sounds in Words

Nina responds well when expectations are clear. She approaches the writing task willingly. She listens to the dictation sentence then begins to write (Figure 2.15).

Nina writes carefully and confidently. She does segment sounds to write words. With many words she writes them as soon as she says them. She knows about how words look and has a strong sense of the relationship between sound and letter. Her writing is primarily in capital letters. She knows the letters (and clusters of letters) in *the* and *stop* but represents them out of sequence. I note her responses to this task as follows:

Figure 2.15: Nina's Hearing and Recording Sounds in Words

Hearing and Recording Sounds in Words

- 35/37 (Stanine 8)
- Confident in her ability to write
- Uses her knowledge of how words look as much as sound to letter
- Orients text to page; control of spaces between letters, spaces between words
- Writes using primarily capital letters
- Next step—lowercase letters.

Figure 2.16 sets out the trends for Hearing and Recording Sounds in Words scores for the class.

HEARING AND RECORDING SOUNDS IN WORDS

Beginning of Year Results

Stanine	1	2	3	4	5	6	7	8	9
Raw Score Range	0	1	2–4	5–11	12–18	19–26	27–33	34-36	37
# of Students	13	3	5	2	1	0	1	1	0
% of Students	56.52	13.	21.73	8.69	4.34		4.34	4.34	

Figure 2.16: Class Data for Hearing and Recording Sounds in Words

While many children know the names of letters, they are only beginning to hear and record the sounds letters make. Two children have significant sound-letter correspondence and knowledge of words. Thirteen children have no experience with recording sounds.

TASK 5: WORD READING

This task asks children to read a list of words. Children score on the number of words correctly identified from a list of 20 high-frequency words derived from children's books. There are a number of lists teachers may choose to use.

I ask myself about the children's responses:

- Do I see consistency in words students are able to write and words students can read?
- What might I expect as individual children read, based on their strengths in word recognition?

Celia's Word Reading

Celia "reads" color words for each word. She is confident in her approximations. After she has exhausted all the colors she can think of, I note her response to this task as follows:

Word Reading

- Word Reading 0 (Stanine 1)
- Approximates confidently by stating color words
- Next step—reading name.

Julio's Word Reading

Julio reads the word *I*. I note his response to this task as follows:

Word Reading

- Word Reading 1 (Stanine 3)
- Read word *I*
- Next step—increase high-frequency words.

Nina's Word Reading

Nina reads four words; *I, is, no,* and *can.* She had written *can* in the Writing Words task and had used the word *is* in the Hearing and Recording Words task. I suspect that she may know more words than she read, but she appeared concerned by the size of the list even when using a marker for reading. I note Nina's responses to this task as follows:

Word Reading

- Word Reading 4/23 (Stanine 5)
- Knows *I, is, no, can*
- Next step—further identification of known words.

Figure 2.17 sets out the class trends for Word Reading.

The information collected from the Word Reading task is confirmation of the Writing Vocabulary data. Over 90% of the students are not familiar with reading and writing words, yet most children made close attempts to write their names.

WORD READING

Beginning of Year Results

Stanine	1	2	3	4	5	6	7	8	9
Raw Score Range	0	0	1	2–3	4–7	8–13	4–19	20–22	23
# of Students	14 →		7	0	2	0	0	0	0
% of Students	60.86		30.43		8.69				

Figure 2.17: Class Data for Word Reading

TASK 6: RECORDING ORAL READING

This assessment freeze frames reading behavior and allows me to analyze those behaviors away from the child. Oral reading behaviors can be recorded and analyzed using conventions designed by Marie Clay (2002). These standard conventions as descriptions of reading behaviors with their analysis allow me to compare reading behaviors over time, make instructional decisions, and share this information with parents and colleagues.

I ask these questions about the child's oral reading behaviors:

- What can the child do and what is the child attempting to do?
- What do these young readers show me about how they handle text?

Does the child know where to begin? What responses occur when I introduce the book? Does the child use pictures as a source of information? Is the child trying to make sense out of what has been put in front of him or her? How does the child use oral language to support the meaning being made? Is the child attending to letters, sounds, and words? Is there any evidence of word-by-word matching?

- What does the child need to learn next?

Celia's Oral Reading

I note how Celia approaches the text. I talk about the cover. "The name of this book is *I Can Read* (Malcolm 1996). It's about a girl who reads to all the different people in her house. Let's open the book and see whom she reads to. We'll read the first page together. 'I can read to Mum.' " Celia reads with me and smiles. "Now you read the next page," I say. Celia looks at the next page and reads, "The girl and Daddy." She continues inventing the text throughout the rest of the book. She does not look at the print, but is very engaged in the pictures. She turns the pages and sometimes begins with the picture on the right page, while other times, she begins with the picture on the left page. She is delighted with herself at the end of the book. "I do this too!" she says, pointing to the girl on the cover. I record her oral reading as shown in Figure 2.18.

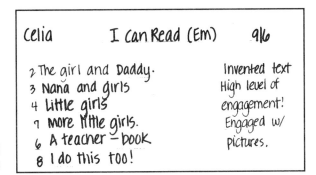

Figure 2.18: Oral Reading Record on Celia

I note her responses to oral reading as follows:

Oral Reading

- Continues to make meaning of the story
- Uses pictures as a source of information
- Invents text based on picture
- Turns pages
- Alternates where to begin when reading (sometimes left page, sometimes right)
- Enjoys the experience ("I do this too!" pointing to the girl reading on the cover)
- Next step—left to right.

Julio's Oral Reading

Julio is enthusiastic about reading the book. I provide the same introduction for him as for Celia. We read the first page together. He reads as shown in Figure 2.19.

Julio immediately picks up on the pattern of the text and uses the initial pattern inserting his natural language where it makes sense. On each page, he puts his finger under the word *I* and says, "This is *I*." He slides his finger underneath the print, but does not attend closely to individual words. I note his responses to the oral reading as follows:

- Knows reading should make sense
- Uses pattern of book as a support
- Uses natural language as a support, confirms knowledge of word *I*

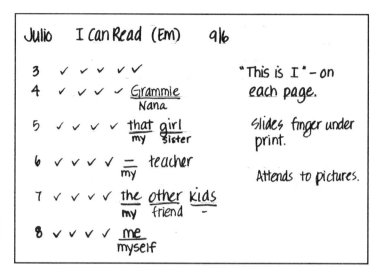

Figure 2.19: Oral
Reading Record
on Julio

- Uses pictures as a source of information
- Approximates with word-by-word matching (Note: Can read word *I* in isolation and in context but does not write it)
- Next step—word-by-word matching.

Nina's Oral Reading

Nina's book is *The Fox* (Boland 1996), a text that is at her stage of reading development.

As shown in Figure 2.20, Nina is able to read more complex texts than Celia and Julio. Where did she use meaning? Where did she use the structure of language? Where did she use the visual source of information? What did she do when she came upon a challenge as she read?

I notice that Nina is not sacrificing meaning at all when she reads, even when she comes upon a challenge. Each word she substitutes makes sense within the structure of the sentence and the story. My analysis shows me that she is asking the questions, "Does it make sense and does it sound right?" when she makes a substitution. Her next step is to ask herself the question, "Does it look right?" and begin to monitor her reading by attending more to the print. I note Nina's response to the oral reading task as follows:

Oral Reading

- *The Fox* (88% accuracy)
- Uses pattern to support reading

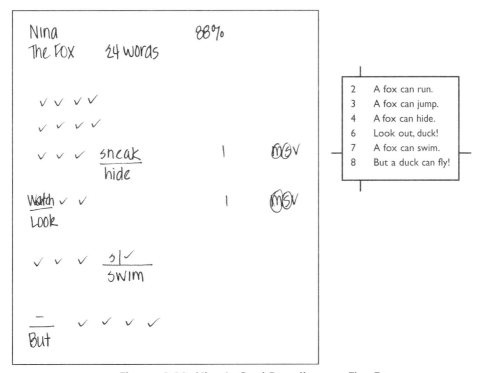

Figure 2.20: Nina's Oral Reading on *The Fox*

- Makes meaningful substitutions
- Next step—self-correction using visual information.

There are three recognized stages of reading development that help me monitor my students along the literacy continuum: emergent, early, and fluent. Margaret Mooney, in the *Books for Young Learners Teacher Resource* (Mooney 2003) and *Literacy Learning: Teachers as Professional Decision Makers Resource Book* (2004), has characterized these stages for readers, writers, and speakers. These characteristics for emergent and early 1 stages are set out in Appendix B.

In my classroom, I use the leveling system from the **Books for Young Learners Collection,** which I match to Mooney's Characteristics of Learners (Appendix C) to help me think about my students' developmental levels. This enables me to identify a child's placement on a literacy continuum. As each student's literacy learning improves, he or she moves through the emergent stage into the early stage on the literacy continuum where I expect the majority to be by the end of kindergarten.

Figure 2.21 shows the progress of my class at the beginning of the year.

RECORD OF ORAL READING

Beginning of the Year Results

Stage of Development	Emergent	Early 1	Early 2	Early 3	Early 4
# of Students	21	2	0	0	0
% of Students	91.31	8.69			

Figure 2.21: Trends in Oral Reading

The majority of the class is at the emergent stage on the literacy continuum measured by their oral reading. I understand that within this emergent stage there are children with a wide range of literacy experiences. Some will have a well-developed literacy set, some will not.

From the oral reading data I have collected, I can make an evaluation of the child's progress. The questions are not different from the questions used for any evaluation. What can this reader do? What is the reader attempting to do? What does this reader need to learn next? This evaluation of oral reading at the emergent stage is focused on the developing behaviors of the literacy set. I'm looking for evidence of growing knowledge of book handling skills, word-by-word matching, and paying attention to print. As the skills of the emergent reader are consolidated, I begin to look for opportunities further along the continuum. The evaluation of oral reading then focuses on the sources of information that readers use. Do their errors make sense and sound right? Are they visually similar? Is the child making sense of what he or she is reading even though it is not word perfect?

DEVELOPING A SYSTEM FOR MONITORING LEARNING

The information collected confirms what I expected from the beginning. This is a group of diverse children. Their needs reach across a large spectrum of literacy learning. The tools I use provide me that information. I have evidence of the strengths and next steps for each child.

My data must be organized for me to use it effectively. How do I record what I currently know? How do I develop a system for keeping track of student learning across the year? Chapter 3 looks at how I organize data to monitor student learning.

3 monitoring student learning

The time spent administering the Observation Survey, discussion in small groups with *My Book,* gathering information from caregivers about the literacy and cultural experiences of the home, and observing the child interacting in the classroom have given me a wealth of starting points for the new learning of individuals in my class. The question I ask myself now is, "How do I manage the data that show me my students are learning?"

Data lets me determine what they know about reading and writing. I need to organize that information and make connections with what the school wants them to know (Cazden 1992). I expect my instruction to result in new learning. As part of my monitoring, I need a system that shows evidence that learning occurs over time.

DEVELOPING THE LITERACY RECORD

I understand that a well-developed literacy set is a predictor of learning success for a child. I know where each individual child is on a continuum of literacy learning, and I need a system for continuing to record learning as it occurs. The Literacy Record is a tool that allows me to record what students know when they enter kindergarten and what they learn throughout the year. The front of the record is illustrated in Figure 3.1. It sets out the essential attitudes, skills, and behaviors that form a well-developed literacy set and provides space for the teacher to record evidence of these behaviors becoming part of a student's learning. Figure 3.2 shows the back of the record, where a teacher records oral reading development.

The Literacy Record

Child's Name _____ Date of Birth _____

DEVELOPMENT OF ATTITUDES	BEHAVIORS TO OBSERVE	DATE observed	repeated	established
Enjoys writing	Seeks involvement and becomes engaged			
Enjoys reading	Seeks involvement and becomes engaged			
Expects writing to make sense	Rereads to confirm meaning			
Enjoys rhyme and rhythm of language	Uses book language in retelling Uses book language in writing (Once upon a time ...)			
DEVELOPMENT OF ATTITUDES	**BEHAVIORS TO OBSERVE**	**DATE** observed	repeated	established
Front and back of book	Automatically starts at front of book (trade and own published books)			
Left to right and return sweep	Reads left to right with return sweep Writes left to right with return sweep			
Word-by-word matching	Can match finger, voice, print in trade and own books Articulates difference between a letter and a word			
Pictures as a source of information	Uses pictures in reading to prompt anticipation and prediction			
Structure of a story	Uses structure in writing			
Concept of a word	Has control over a number of words in writing and reading			
Letters of a word are written in a sequence	Recognizes, can read and write own name and some other words			
Features of text	Can identify and use some punctuation in reading and writing			
Speech sounds can be written as letters	Approximates spelling in writing using consistent sound/letter (Underline or highlight when student is consistent)	A B C D E F G H I J K L M N O P Q R S T U V W X Y Z a a b c d e f g g h i j k l m n o p q r s t u v w x y z		
Printed words have letters represented by sounds	Uses visual information to relate letter to initial sound in reading			
Letter form generalizations Upper- and lowercase letters	Uses letters of alphabet in writing Recognizes letters of alphabet (Underline or highlight when student is consistent)	A B C D E F G H I J K L M N O P Q R S T U V W X Y Z a a b c d e f g g h i j k l m n o p q r s t u v w x y z		

front

Figure 3.1: The Literacy Record—Front

The Literacy Record

Child's Name _____ Date of Birth _____

DATE	TEXT	RECORD OF ORAL READING	SUMMARY STATEMENT
	SP TB	Title	
	SP TB	Title	
	SP TB	Title	
	SP TB	Title	
	SP TB	Title	
	SP TB	Title	
	SP TB	Title	

KEY   SP   **Student published**
          TB   **Trade book**

Available from Richard C. Owen Publishers, Inc.
PO Box 585 • Katonah, New York 10536 • Orders: 800-262-0787 • www.RCOwen.com
Created by Marilyn Duncan. © 2005 by Richard C. Owen Publishers, Inc. All rights reserved.

back

Figure 3.2: The Literacy Record—Back

The Literacy Record becomes a summary of the developing literacy behaviors that lead to competency as readers and writers. While reading and writing comprise the key aspects of the record, literacy development is observable as children listen, speak, view, and present.

Baseline data gathered from the Observation Survey, *My Book,* and my observational notes help me plan for the whole class. I can identify learning patterns. I can see how many children understand directionality and word-by-word matching. What needs might I meet through whole group instruction? Can I see opportunities for small group instruction? I note that six children need to learn about the front and back of the books. I note also, there are some individuals who have unique needs.

USING THE LITERACY RECORD

When a specific reading behavior is first observed, such as a child following print from left to right, a note is made and dated. A second date is recorded when the behavior is repeated. A third date is recorded when the behavior is seen consistently and firmly established, as illustrated in Figure 3.3.

DEVELOPMENT OF ATTITUDES	BEHAVIORS TO OBSERVE	DATE observed	repeated	established
Front and back of book	Automatically starts at front of book (trade and own published books)	9|6	9|11	9|21

Figure 3.3: Example of Recording Information on the Literacy Record

I record each child's oral reading on the Literacy Record at least every three weeks. I use trade books and the student's own writing in their student-published books. These records provide evidence of growth over time and reflect exactly what understandings children develop as they read. Space is provided on the oral reading record for a monitoring note, summarizing the behaviors observed. This summary statement focuses on behaviors of emergent readers, as noted on the front of the record.

Using the Literacy Record allows me to use my time effectively because I know what to teach. I can also keep my expectations high since I am focused on what to observe.

DATE	TEXT	RECORD OF ORAL READING	SUMMARY STATEMENT
10/1	(SP) TB	Title The New Car	Story makes sense . L to R Return sweep Next step: word-by-word matching

Figure 3.4: Example of Completed Record of Oral Reading

The Literacy Record

Child's Name *Celia* _____ Date of Birth _____

DEVELOPMENT OF ATTITUDES	BEHAVIORS TO OBSERVE	DATE observed	repeated	established
Enjoys writing	Seeks involvement and becomes engaged	9/6		
Enjoys reading	Seeks involvement and becomes engaged			
Expects writing to make sense	Rereads to confirm meaning			
Enjoys rhyme and rhythm of language	Uses book language in retelling Uses book language in writing (Once upon a time ...)			

DEVELOPMENT OF ATTITUDES	BEHAVIORS TO OBSERVE	DATE observed	repeated	established
Front and back of book	Automatically starts at front of book (trade and own published books)			
Left to right and return sweep	Reads left to right with return sweep Writes left to right with return sweep			
Word-by-word matching	Can match finger, voice, print in trade and own books Articulates difference between a letter and a word			
Pictures as a source of information	Uses pictures in reading to prompt anticipation and prediction			
Structure of a story	Uses structure in writing			
Concept of a word	Has control over a number of words in writing and reading			
Letters of a word are written in a sequence	Recognizes, can read and write own name and some other words			
Features of text	Can identify and use some punctuation in reading and writing			
Speech sounds can be written as letters	Approximates spelling in writing using consistent sound/letter (Underline or highlight when student is consistent)	A B C D E F G H I J K L M N O P Q R S T U V W X Y Z a a b c d e f g g h i j k l m n o p q r s t u v w x y z		
Printed words have letters represented by sounds	Uses visual information to relate letter to initial sound in reading			
Letter form generalizations Upper- and lowercase letters	Uses letters of alphabet in writing Recognizes letters of alphabet (Underline or highlight when student is consistent)	A B Ⓒ D E F G H I J K L M N O P Q R S T U V W X Y Z a a b c d e f g g h i j k l m n o p q r s t u v w x y z		

front

Figure 3.5: Celia's Literacy Record—Front

The Literacy Record

Child's Name _Celia_   Date of Birth _____

DATE	TEXT	RECORD OF ORAL READING	SUMMARY STATEMENT
	SP (TB)	Title _I can Read_ _EM_	_Uses pictures as source of information._ _Invents text based on pictures._ _Turns pages._ _Next step: Where to start, L to R._

Figure 3.6: Celia's Literacy Record—Partial Back of Form

USING WHAT I HAVE LEARNED

Baseline information that I have on the Literacy Record about individual learners enables me to look for patterns in their literacy behaviors and then to determine what they need to learn next. With this information I can group for initial instruction. I have set out the Literacy Records of Celia, Julio, and Nina suggesting what they already know and can do; what I would expect they need to do next; and how as a teacher I would provide the kinds of experiences that ensure they learn. I have records of 20 other students. Figures 3.5 and 3.6 set out Celia's Literacy Record with the data from the Observation Survey, *My Book,* and other observations of her literacy learning.

Note the entry on the Literacy Record that shows Celia's knowledge of the letter *C* and her attitude toward learning to speak, read, and write. Celia needs to continue the development of her literacy set. It is difficult to always work with her alone, so how am I going to provide support through grouping and regrouping her with other students? What other children in my classroom have similar needs? What instructional approaches might I use?

From the Observation Survey data, Celia and seven other children need to learn more about the alphabet. Instruction will be required throughout the day using a variety of approaches. Their names are meaningful and important to them and are words they will be able to write and read. Their own names will be the start of their reading and writing vocabulary.

Celia and thirteen other children need support in understanding how books work. Six children need the skill of identifying the front and back of a book and knowing where to begin to read. All need repeated exposure to books, through being read to them or through the use of audio tapes. These children should also be involved in ongoing conversations about books; they need opportunities to "play at reading" and to be in the book area of the classroom with books they have had read to them and with books they are anxious to explore. They need to be encouraged to tell stories, with the flannel board and with puppets.

Support in developing understanding of how books work can happen every day through their own daily writing. I will publish their writing by producing a correct copy of what they have written in a little book. They can then read what they have written (see Chapter 9).

Julio's Literacy Record in Figures 3.7 and 3.8 shows that he has some development of a literacy set. What support does he need to continue this development? Are there others in the classroom requiring similar support?

Julio has already shown his ability to learn letter names and retain that knowledge, so clearing up confusions and learning new letters will probably be easy for him. This strength in his oral language, combined with his letter knowledge, means he will be a support to other children working independently in the alphabet area.

It is important to build on the confidence Julio has about handling books. Because of his enthusiasm for books and stories, he will be a good model for children in the book area who are beginning to "play at reading." In the Concepts About Print and oral reading tasks, he demonstrated awareness of directionality. Learning word-by-word matching can occur in small group instruction with other children who also need that skill.

It is important for Julio and other children to gain the same confidence in writing that they show in reading. Writing daily, and publishing their writing as small books that can be read and reread, will show them that being a reader and a speaker can be helpful as a writer. Confidence comes by understanding that stories told and sketches drawn can help a writer write and that these stories can be read by the writer and also read by others.

Labeling objects around the room enables children to link objects they identify with words they can begin to learn. Encouraging them to label materials they need to use (such as the location of crayons, pencils, books), or things they build and make, supports other children as well.

Julio will learn some things in the whole group, others through small group instruction, and some with individual support from the teacher.

Nina has a well-developed literacy set. She needs opportunities to be engaged in activities that will allow me to observe some of the skills that I was unable to record through my initial observations. Does she have an understanding of story structure? Is she able to retell a known story? What does she know about book language and the rhyme and rhythm of language? What do I need to see to determine her level of enjoyment as a reader and a writer?

The Literacy Record

Child's Name _Julio_ _____ Date of Birth _____

DEVELOPMENT OF ATTITUDES	BEHAVIORS TO OBSERVE	DATE observed	repeated	established
Enjoys writing	Seeks involvement and becomes engaged	9/6		
Enjoys reading	Seeks involvement and becomes engaged	9/6		
Expects writing to make sense	Rereads to confirm meaning			
Enjoys rhyme and rhythm of language	Uses book language in retelling Uses book language in writing (Once upon a time ...)			

DEVELOPMENT OF ATTITUDES	BEHAVIORS TO OBSERVE	DATE observed	repeated	established
Front and back of book	Automatically starts at front of book (trade and own published books)	9/6		
Left to right and return sweep	Reads left to right with return sweep Writes left to right with return sweep	9/6		
Word-by-word matching	Can match finger, voice, print in trade and own books Articulates difference between a letter and a word			
Pictures as a source of information	Uses pictures in reading to prompt anticipation and prediction	9/6		
Structure of a story	Uses structure in writing			
Concept of a word	Has control over a number of words in writing and reading			
Letters of a word are written in a sequence	Recognizes, can read and write own name and some other words			
Features of text	Can identify and use some punctuation in reading and writing			
Speech sounds can be written as letters	Approximates spelling in writing using consistent sound/letter (Underline or highlight when student is consistent)	A B C D E F G H I J K L M N O P Q R S T U V W X Y Z a a b c d e f g g h i j k l m n o p q r s t u v w x y z		
Printed words have letters represented by sounds	Uses visual information to relate letter to initial sound in reading			
Letter form generalizations Upper- and lowercase letters	Uses letters of alphabet in writing Recognizes letters of alphabet (Underline or highlight when student is consistent)	A B C D E F G H I J K L M _all_ N O P Q R S T U V W X Y Z @ (a) b (c) d (e) f (g) g h (i) (j) (k) (l) m n (o) (p) q r (s) (t) (u) (v) (w) (x) (y) (z)		

front

Figure 3.7: Julio's Literacy Record—Front

The Literacy Record

Child's Name _Julio_   Date of Birth _____

DATE	TEXT	RECORD OF ORAL READING	SUMMARY STATEMENT
	SP (TB)	Title _I can Read_ _EM_	_Knows reading should make sense._ _Uses patterns as support. Knows "I"_ _Next step: Word-by-word matching_

Figure 3.8: Julio's Literacy Record—Partial Back of Form

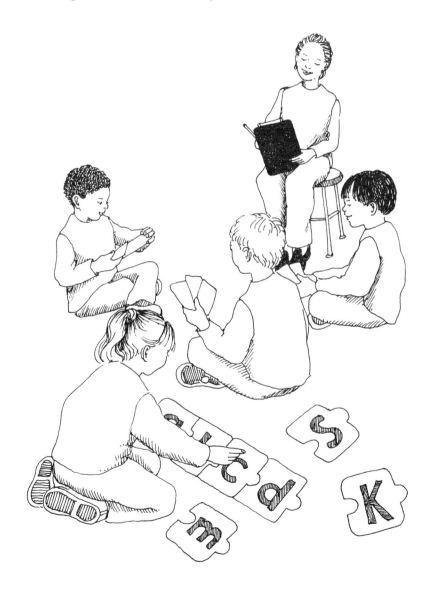

The Literacy Record

Child's Name _Nina_ _____ Date of Birth _____

DEVELOPMENT OF ATTITUDES	BEHAVIORS TO OBSERVE	DATE observed	repeated	established
Enjoys writing	Seeks involvement and becomes engaged	9/6		
Enjoys reading	Seeks involvement and becomes engaged			
Expects writing to make sense	Rereads to confirm meaning			
Enjoys rhyme and rhythm of language	Uses book language in retelling Uses book language in writing (Once upon a time ...)	9/6		

DEVELOPMENT OF ATTITUDES	BEHAVIORS TO OBSERVE	DATE observed	repeated	established
Front and back of book	Automatically starts at front of book (trade and own published books)	————————		9/6
Left to right and return sweep	Reads left to right with return sweep Writes left to right with return sweep			
Word-by-word matching	Can match finger, voice, print in trade and own books Articulates difference between a letter and a word	———————— ————————		9/6 9/6
Pictures as a source of information	Uses pictures in reading to prompt anticipation and prediction			
Structure of a story	Uses structure in writing			
Concept of a word	Has control over a number of words in writing and reading			
Letters of a word are written in a sequence	Recognizes, can read and write own name and some other words	————————		9/6
Features of text	Can identify and use some punctuation in reading and writing			
Speech sounds can be written as letters	Approximates spelling in writing using consistent sound/letter (Underline or highlight when student is consistent)	A B C D E F G H I J K L M N O P Q R S T U V W X Y Z a a b c d e f g g h i j k l m n o p q r s t u v w x y z		
Printed words have letters represented by sounds	Uses visual information to relate letter to initial sound in reading			
Letter form generalizations Upper- and lowercase letters	Uses letters of alphabet in writing Recognizes letters of alphabet (Underline or highlight when student is consistent)	A B C D E F G H I J K L M _all_ N O P Q R S T U V W X Y Z a a b c d e f g g h i j k l m n o p q r s t u v w x y z		

front

Figure 3.9: Nina's Literacy Record—Front

The Literacy Record

Child's Name *Nina* _____ Date of Birth _____

DATE	TEXT	RECORD OF ORAL READING	SUMMARY STATEMENT
9/6	SP (TB)	Title *The Fox EI*	*Uses pattern to support reading.* *Makes meaningful substitutions.* *Next step: Use additional sources of* *of information to sc (visual)*

Figure 3.10: Nina's Literacy Record—Partial Back of Form

While Nina is at a different stage of development than many of the learners in the classroom, I see opportunities for her to be in groups with other children because of similar needs. Her confusions about first and last parts of the story, page, line, and first and last word in a sentence indicate lack of skills other children need to develop also. Her facility with language means she will be a great addition to a group, while also learning what she needs to know next.

Nina will also benefit from being in mixed groups with more verbal children for discussions of wordless texts. She knows about books and they know about the expression of ideas; they will learn from each other.

I note one other child has a similar level of experience with reading and writing as Nina. There are times when I will meet with the two of them. Both children make meaningful predictions and substitutions as they read, but they have not yet demonstrated any self-correcting behaviors. I expect to build on their strength by providing instruction that will foster and develop that skill with resources that offer sufficient challenges for their learning.

MONITORING GROWTH OVER TIME

The Literacy Record is a summary of student learning. It shows evidence of children applying what they have learned. The back of The Literacy Record highlights the importance of information recorded when the child reads orally. Two other tools are used to gather learning data—the student's draft writing book, and notes I record throughout the day about individual students. The remainder of this chapter explores how those two tools are used to monitor learning.

The Draft Writing Book

Each child has a draft writing book. Its purposes are to keep a student's writing in one place and to show a date for each writing entry so I can monitor writing growth over time. Through my observations of writing, I note how students select a topic, organize their thinking with a pencil sketch, write down their thoughts, and I observe the learner's control over sounds and letters and essential words for writing.

The Essential Word List

The 290 essential words for writing and reading identify the high-frequency words students are expected to know by the end of grade 2 (Croft 1998). Children who write daily in kindergarten naturally use many of these words. Their ability to increase the number of words they can write fluently and automatically will support them in reading as well as in their writing. A cumulative "Words I Know" list can be kept in their writing draft book or a writing folder, as shown in Figure 3.11 (Mooney 2004b). Further discussion of essential words can be found in Chapters 8 and 9 and the entire list appears in Appendix E.

I record evidence of the sounds, letters, and essential words the child is learning and using (Figure 3.12). This can be placed in the back of the child's draft writing book. (The full page is in Appendix B.)

The three charts, concerning consonants and diagraphs, vowels, and essential words, form the core of word skill development. The consonant and diagraph chart enables me to record both the letter-name knowledge and corresponding sound. When students are learning short vowels, they use their knowledge of high-frequency words to support them. The essential word list records the child's developing mastery of the 290 words used most frequently in reading and writing. These words have to be learned quickly and accurately as a critical component of the child's literacy development.

Learning to write is learning to create. Part of learning to write is learning that writers write for readers. To help students make sense of what they write, I need to know what a child understands about the writing process: how topics are selected, what links are seen between a sketch as a plan for writing, how clearly their writing records their thoughts, and a clear and accurate record of their word skill development. The notes I record on these aspects of writing development can be on the last few pages of the child's draft book. They need to be brief yet meaningful and will become part of a comprehensive profile of each child's development as a writer.

Words I Know

a at all am and	b be big baby	c can come	d dog do did Dad
e eat	f from for fun	g go get got	h he his him
i I is in it	j just	k keep	l little let love
m me my Mom	n no not	o on of off	p put play
q quack	r run red	s see she so sun	t to the they
u up us	v very	w we went will	x
y you yes	z		

Figure 3.11: A "Words I Know" List

MONITORING—LETTERS, SOUNDS, WORDS

Consonants and Diagraphs

	Letter Name	Letter Formation		Taught Sound	Used	Maintained
		UC	LC			
b						
c						
d						
f						
g						
h						
j						
k						
l						
m						

Vowels

	Letter Name	Letter Formation		Taught Sound	Used	Maintained
		UC	LC			
a at						
e end						
i it						
o on						
u up						

ESSENTIAL WORDS

Word	Taught	Maintained

Figure 3.12: Evidence of Learning (Partial Form) Goes in Back of Child's Draft Writing Book

MONITORING INDIVIDUALS IN SMALL GROUPS

Like writing, reading is about the creation of meaning. Readers need to make sense of what others have written. Reading is comprehension. To comprehend, children need to know how language works and how letters and sounds interact.

To record the essential aspects of reading development, I have a folder for each child. Clipped to the front of the folder is The Literacy Record, with the summary of the child's oral reading laid out in front of me. The 23 folders reveal patterns that lead instructional decisions. For example, I note that most children are making predictions as they read but do not yet confirm the predictions. I know I can support learning that skill by whole-group demonstrations.

I record notes from my observation of student learning during small literacy groups. For example, from my review of folders laid out in front of me, I find four children who need to confirm their predictions by using the print. With that as my objective, I will meet with the group over the next few weeks to develop that skill. Figure 3.13 illustrates where I will record the result of this small group instruction on a sheet of sticky notes. When I have information about each child, I peel the sticky note from the sheet and place it in the child's individual folder.

Figure 3.13: Monitoring Progress During Literacy Groups

Objective:
To confirm predictions using text.

Charles
Confirms with initial sounds

Anna
Approx. based on meaning—needs support to think beyond obvious

Julio
Confirms with phrases— "see it says - in the house - that told me where."

Celeste Confirms with known words (that's dog - that's my spelling word)

It is important that I monitor each individual's ability to apply his or her new skills in other situations. Is evidence of the child's learning about language structures in reading also appearing in their writing and speaking? This information is in the folder, as well as illustrated by the recorded notes in Figure 3.14.

Figure 3.14: Individual Monitoring

> **Name:** Alberto   **Date:** Dec. 3
>
> Uses book language to retell
> "This cereal is just right - not hot, not cold."

It is easy to become overwhelmed by the complexity of behaviors that need to be monitored and recorded. Effectively monitoring the learning of my students is a skill that requires perseverance, practice, and planning. It is important to begin with a few students and to monitor them systematically on one or two aspects of reading and writing. For example, I may begin by monitoring five children daily in the classroom library to determine if they are applying left-to-right and return sweep. Once observation and recording become more automatic, I can add more children to the system.

Focusing my observations on key reading and writing behaviors is important. Equally important is the need to be aware of other aspects of literacy development. For example, during small group reading instruction, I can also assess the child's ability to listen or any increases in vocabulary. I watch for the child to return to that book selection after the group is over. I must be open to the development of literacy in all of its forms and throughout my classroom.

HOW DO I MANAGE THE LEARNING OF 23 TO 50 CHILDREN?

The data I am collecting confirms that this is a group of diverse children, and their needs reach across the spectrum of literacy learning. These children are learners waiting for someone to release their potential! I need to know my tools and how to use them.

I know what I need to collect about these children. I observe intentionally and perceptively. I make professional judgments about the information so I can plan appropriate instruction. I expect that my instruction will result in student learning, which in turn will require further data gathering, observation, recording, and instructional decisions.

Next, I face the bigger question. Now that I know what they know and what they need, how will I organize the classroom? What learning areas will support these children? What materials will support their learning? What expectations will I set for their independent access to these learning spaces and these materials? If I am going to meet with small groups and individuals, how will others manage their time? In Chapter 4 we explore how the environment is organized to support learning.

4 learning spaces

ORGANIZING LEARNING SPACES

The classroom environment is organized for learning. Spaces are arranged to enable learning to occur easily and naturally: spaces for the whole class to gather for demonstrations, and spaces to work with small groups. Teachers need easy access to move around the room with individual children.

There is a need for spaces where children can practice skills they have learned, spaces to talk, to work quietly, and spaces low enough to explore and engaging enough to entice a five year old to sit and work. Kindergartens sometimes have "learning centers" where children engage in activities the teacher designs or a program provides. Centers are intended to keep children busy and to manage their learning behavior, but students make few decisions and work at the level and the pace of the "learning center" program.

An environment that promotes learning becomes a workplace for five year olds, a place that will nurture academic, personal, and social growth. While the environment is predictable and orderly, it is also challenging. It allows for the natural interactions among children that foster growth. They learn to get along and resolve conflicts. The classroom organization is intentional, and it supports literacy development because children talk to one another. It's important to create a classroom that is a center for learning rather than a classroom of learning centers. The predictability of a classroom as a center for learning promotes independence because the children understand how the workplace works. There is never a surprise in the work space they move to next. For example, I may add new books for children to read, but the children always know they will independently read in this space.

In a classroom organized as a center for learning, work spaces encourage independent work in reading, learning about the alphabet, poems, rhymes, songs and jingles, listening, writing, art and illustrations, as well as spaces for spelling, handwriting, investigation, and storytelling.

A Space for Reading

Reading is about engaging with text. Reading instruction begins when children like and value books. Good attitudes about books form when young children enjoy the same story over and over again. Young children like to "own" stories. When they do, they read, reread, and then read again, whether or not they read the words accurately. They read to themselves, to adults, to their toys, and they read to friends. They bring all they know to reading: their expectations, their knowledge of language structure, their ability to predict, their understanding of how books and print work, their understanding of how illustrations support a reader, their knowledge of how to use the print, and their beginning understandings of how these things work together to create meaning.

Children need to explore books and have a place to do it. Access to books enables them to figure out what the book is about, to study illustrations, wonder, learn new words, pose questions, and to find answers. Children need time to "play" at reading, to practice what they know and to learn new things, to share with their classmates, and to talk about what they read.

The reading space and classroom library should allow children to tuck up with a book. Soft cushions and private corners encourage involvement with books. In the reading space, bookshelves are low enough for the child to see the covers of books. Posters and other wall text are at a child's height. A wide range of high-quality books is available, including new books and old favorites in a variety of genres, organized so a child can select and return them to the correct place.

The book space is busy but lacks real noise. Kindergarten children talk about what they are reading, what they have read, and they read aloud. They share books with one another and tell stories from the pictures. They laugh at funny parts.

The library space has a place for the children's published writing. These books are published by the teacher (see Chapter 8). They become independent reading material for the emergent reader. The child who wrote the story "owns" it, understands it, and can delight in reading it to him- or herself or anyone who will listen.

Observing children in the reading space, a teacher might ask, "What can this child do? What learning is occurring as he or she explores books?" There are two things expected of children in the classroom library: to explore books they cannot yet read, and to practice reading at their independent level.

With children who are exploring books, teachers look for certain formative behaviors:

- Developing oral language skills through "playing at reading"
- Using pictures as a source of information
- Practicing book handling skills.

At the independent level, the following behaviors would be observed:

- Employing skills they have been taught on materials they can read easily
- Approximating skills they are learning
- Acquiring new skills
- Developing fluency.

A Space for Learning about the Alphabet

Children are attracted to learning about alphabet letters: naming them, examining the shapes of letters, their differences, and how they can be put together to make words. The talk that accompanies their discoveries is important to literacy development. Just as students will try what is demonstrated, they will talk about it. They learn from each other.

The alphabet space includes magnetic letters, plastic letters, wooden letters, alphabet books, games and puzzles, whiteboards, and markers. Alphabet friezes are on the walls at the child's height. Letters and familiar pictures including photographs of the children and their names show how sounds are connected to letters.

What are teachers observing about student learning in the alphabet space? Students are:

- Acquiring knowledge of letters and sounds
- Relating sounds and symbols
- Manipulating letters to make words.

As in the reading space, observations would be recorded and become part of the data used for instructional planning.

A Space for Poems, Rhymes, Songs, and Jingles

Children enjoy rhyme and rhythm. Reading and reciting well-known poems, jingles, songs, and rhymes provide opportunities to hear and practice the sounds of language. Rhyme and repetition encourage listening to the sounds of words and learning how language works. Rhyme, rhythm, and repetition are important components of phonological awareness.

In this space, favorite poems are reproduced on easily handled cards. Nursery rhymes, finger-plays, jingles, and songs are on charts displayed at the reading height for children. Pointers (just like the teacher uses) are available to practice word-by-word matching. Familiar poems are cut into chunks and pieces so the children can assemble them on the floor or in pocket charts. Small tape recorders, CD players, and headsets let children listen to these familiar songs, rhymes, and poetry.

What are teachers observing about student learning in the poetry space?

Students are:

- Developing oral language, listening, and phonemic awareness skills through listening to—and repetitive reading of—songs, poems, and jingles
- Presenting songs, poems, and jingles
- Practicing word-by-word matching and sequence.

A Space for Listening

Listening repeatedly to the same stories consolidates learning. The more opportunities children have to listen to books being read, the more opportunities they have to discover new things. Children listen and observe as they did when learning to talk. Recorded stories develop discrimination skills: listening for the inflections of the reader, looking at the illustrations and print, and following along.

Materials in this space include a listening post with tape recorders, CD players and headsets with appropriate tapes, CDs, and books and other texts that allow children to follow along and read with voice support.

What are teachers observing about student learning in the listening space? Students are:

- Increasing their experiences of a variety of texts and text forms
- Increasing their vocabulary
- Practicing concepts about print through repeated reading
- Interpreting meaning through expressive language of reader
- Following step-by-step directions
- Developing motor skills about how technology works.

A Space for Writing

Learning to be a writer begins with making marks on paper, a letter mailed to Grandma, a shopping list taken to the supermarket. Writing activities are learned from adult models. Students require an environment where they can explore form, shape, and layout, as they experiment with pencil and paper. They can talk with each other about what they are writing. They can watch other children as they write. They can learn to write by becoming a writer.

In the writing space, the tools for writing are easily accessible. Writing paper is available in a variety of sizes and forms. Practice makes a writer. Children are expected to write daily in their draft writing book. Each entry is dated, and the book becomes a record of growth over time. See Chapters 6, 7, and 8 for further discussion about writing.

Figure 4.1 illustrates Tim's writing at the beginning of the year. There are a number of things Tim can do with the teacher's support. Note the date at the top of the page and a line drawn to separate a place for sketching from the place for writing. Tim has drawn a pencil sketch of himself and his bike. This is what his story is about. Tim can already work independently in the writing space. He can talk about his story with others; he can share what he knows about writing. His talking and writing go hand in hand. He is becoming a writer.

What are teachers observing about student learning in the writing space? Students are:

- Using and practicing the skills they have been taught
- Approximating new skills
- Acquiring skills as they choose a variety of topics, sketching to plan, and recording sounds, letters, and words
- Developing fluency in writing
- Exploring the materials writers use.

Figure 4.1: I rode my bike.

A Space for Illustration

Children use a sketch to get their ideas down as a plan for writing. Talking about their sketch with others expands their ideas. Completed writing is published. When teachers talk about published writing, they mean the corrected text that is made public to its intended audience. Children quickly learn the difference between their planning sketch and illustrating their story. An illustration provides color and embellishment. It becomes an additional source of information for a reader. There is further discussion of publishing and developing children's writing in Chapters 8 through 10.

The space set aside in the classroom where children have all the tools to illustrate their published books encourages exploration, design, and experimentation with shape, texture, and color. What are teachers observing about student learning in the illustration space? Students are:

- Illustrating their published writing
- Matching pictures to the text
- Using a variety of media for illustration.

A Space for Spelling and Handwriting

Margaret Meek says that, "Children's language develops with everyday talk. Most of it is directed at getting things done, but there is another kind that emerges when the day is over… the child lying in bed, not expecting attention and talking. If you listen carefully, you will hear attempts to distinguish sounds and practice them. The child whispers, shouts, squeaks, sings, and produces a whole range of sounds which make up words, like a violinist trying out a new instrument" (1982, 33).

In much the same way, children try out spelling. Teachers watch for the way children are approximating the conventional spelling from what they think the word looks and sounds like. Spelling is about trying to get a picture of the word tucked inside the head. Spelling begins with the need to use a number of high-frequency words correctly. These words are introduced as a support to writing (see Chapters 9 and 10 for more information on spelling instruction). Other words are taken from the closest approximation of words they use in their daily writing. What are teachers observing about student learning in the spelling space? Students are:

- Building a bank of known words for reading and writing through practice and use
- Taking responsibility for a practice procedure
- Building fluency in writing.

Part of learning to write fluently is knowing how to form letters. Handwriting instruction becomes part of a daily routine, and the correct formation of letters needs to be practiced. The more practiced letter formation becomes, the more fluent the child's writing becomes, and even kindergarten students can practice their handwriting on their own. What are teachers observing about student learning in the handwriting space? Students are:

- Practicing letter formation
- Practicing spatial relationships
- Building fluency in writing.

A Space for Investigation

Children have lots of questions. Even a child with limited literacy experiences has great questions. The investigation space is used to collect objects and books that support current units of study. Plants and animals might be permanently a part of this space, as students watch for growth and change. Books and models can also answer the "I wonder" questions prompted by guided observations. Magnifying glasses and tweezers encourage children to examine objects more closely. There are treasures too that come to school in children's pockets like rocks, sticks, bugs, leaves, and other things attractive to inquisitive five year olds.

Children should be encouraged to use books to discover more about what they want to find out. Pictures and artifacts support this learning. Children can talk about what they want to know and have discovered. They can record answers to their questions and label their own special finds. They can ask questions and form hypothesis. They can write about what they want others to know.

What are teachers observing about student learning in the investigation space? Students are:

- Acquiring content vocabulary
- Asking and answering questions
- Sharing information
- Linking investigations to texts
- Presenting information through drawing, labeling, and writing
- Creating meaning through observation
- Applying literacy skills to other content areas.

A Space for Storytelling

Children enjoy dramatizing and interpreting their world through play. They become the characters in the story: the teachers, parents, and people they know. They use puppets, flannel board stories, and costumes to tell stories.

Through storytelling, children develop their oral language and presentation skills. As they watch others perform, they learn to interpret meaning through action. Dramatic play encourages children to share, express their thoughts, communicate, and organize.

What are the teachers observing about student learning in the storytelling space? They are:

- Developing expressive and receptive vocabulary
- Understanding story structure and book language
- Making meaning when viewing gestures, facial expressions, and tone of voice
- Presenting meaning through use of gestures, facial expressions, tone of voice.

These six work spaces and their content will change over the course of the year as learning needs change. New books will be added to the reading spaces collection. As children's knowledge and interests grow, different activities in the alphabet spaces provide variety and sustain interest. Teachers who understand that the power of independent learning lies in the ability of children to use what they know to overcome new challenges also know that these challenges can be structured through activities in the spaces set aside for independent work.

How then, in a classroom organized for independent work, is the learning of 23 different five year olds managed? How do students develop good work habits, responsibility, and an ability to work with others in an environment that encourages independence?

SETTING EXPECTATIONS TO PROMOTE RESPONSIBILITY AND INDEPENDENCE

For children, part of working independently in the classroom work spaces involves developing good work habits and behaving responsibly. Responsibility comes from knowing what is expected. Literacy development is on a continuum; work habits and responsibility are at varying stages of development among my children. To begin, they need a very clear picture of what is expected of them in each work space of the classroom, and I require a clear and consistent way of communicating these expectations.

In the following section of the book, I explain how I establish expectations for the various work spaces and the responsibilities I expect to establish. In the classroom library, for example, I expect children to:

- Find a place to read where they will not be interrupted
- Respect others
- Handle books carefully
- Understand how books are organized and put them back where they belong
- Explore books they are not able to read (through playing at reading)
- Read books at their stage of development.

There are procedures teachers can use with the whole class for establishing and communicating expectations. The class is assembled together. The teacher has a chart tablet and markers. The chart is divided in half. On the top of one side the teacher writes YOUR JOB, on the other side, MY JOB. These charts are posted and used to set and monitor expectations. The accompanying sidebar contains an example of a conversation about expectations the teacher wishes to establish in the reading space.

SETTING EXPECTATIONS

TEACHER: When you read books at home, Colin, where do you go?

COLIN: *I get my favorite book and sit on the sofa.*

TEACHER: That's exactly what I do. Find someplace comfortable to sit. Where might be a comfortable place in this room?

COLIN: *Over there.*

TEACHER:	What makes "over there" look comfortable?
COLIN:	*Those pillows. I like that place between the bookshelves, I could take a pillow there. I could lie on my tummy.*
TEACHER:	So I think you have the idea! It's your responsibility to find a comfortable place to read just like you do at home. As you read at home, what do you do next?
COLIN:	*I put the book on my lap and turn the pages.*
TEACHER:	Ah, you know what readers do. That's exactly what I expect you to do when you are in the classroom library.
TEACHER:	I have an idea. The classroom library is one of your jobs, in this kindergarten. Let's make a list of what your job might be.
	Colin, would you show us what it might look like when you are in the classroom library?
	Let's watch Colin. What is he doing first?
MEAGAN:	*He's getting a book.*
TEACHER:	Let's put that on our list. (I write *Choose a book*). Now what is he doing? He's finding a comfortable place to read. I'll write that next. *Find a comfortable place.* Now look. He has the book on his lap and he's started reading. I'll write that. *Read the book.*
TEACHER:	I wonder what he'll do when he's *finished* with that book?
JANISHA:	*Get another one!*
TEACHER:	That's a good idea but what should he do with the book he's just finished reading?
JANISHA:	*He better put it away.*
TEACHER:	You're absolutely right. Show us how that might look, Colin. He's putting it right back on

the shelf where he found it. Let's get that up on the chart.

The teacher directs the students' attention back to the chart and together the class reads about their jobs. The teacher asks the children if it makes sense or if anything has been forgotten.

Your Job	My Job
Choose a book.	
Find a comfortable spot.	
Read your book.	
Put your book away.	

TEACHER: I know that won't be a problem for any of you. Let's practice now.

Four or five children are identified and while they choose books from the classroom library, the other children comment on how they do it.

TEACHER: What do you notice about how Beau is picking his book?

QUENTON: *He takes a couple off the book shelf and then picks one he likes.*

TEACHER: What about the books he's not going to read right now.

QUENTON: *He put them back where he first got them.*

TEACHER: That makes sense, doesn't it? They are there for someone else who might want to read them.

In a short time the whole class reads. The teacher takes this time to observe reading behavior, take a few notes, and at the same time give feedback to children as they read. At the end of this time, the class gathers back in the meeting area and shares the experience. The following is added to the chart.

Your Job	My Job
Choose a book.	Watch children.
Find a comfortable spot.	Listen to children read.
Read your book.	Listen to children tell stories.
Put your book away.	Write down what they can do.

The need for clear expectations is the same for all work spaces in the classroom. The teacher sets expectations for what students can do, but also lets the children know there are expectations for what the teacher does as well.

Monitoring these expectations is just as critical as setting them. Teachers need time to reflect on what is working or not working and to determine why. They need time to observe and to support children in managing themselves within the classroom community. Intervention at the right time helps everyone to get along together.

5 managing the first weeks of school

Kindergarten is not as much preparing for life as it *is* life for a five year old. Children meet and learn to get along with people they don't know. They learn how language works. They learn to ask, to convince, to negotiate, and to explain. They learn to be patient. They have to wait to talk, wait to use the listening post, and wait for the swing on the playground. They learn responsibility and respectfulness. They are expected to be responsible for their belongings, to respect others and things around them.

LIFE AND THE ESSENTIAL SKILLS

As a center for learning, the classroom is a workplace where children learn the skills of literacy, mathematics, and content subjects. As they learn from their schooling how to communicate, how to manipulate numbers and abstract symbols, and how to find information from books and other media, they also learn a set of essential skills that people need in order to live happily in the world around them. They learn how to solve problems for themselves, how to manage time and responsibilities, how to be social and cooperative, how to develop good work and study habits, and how to look after themselves by keeping safe and healthy. The way the classroom is organized helps manage the development of these skills and children become more responsible and able to manage themselves in this environment.

In a classroom where development is focused on these life skills, stickers and material rewards or even behavior management programs are unimportant because children are continually encouraged to develop a strong sense of self and self-worth through what they see themselves and others achieving. This environment encourages learning how to learn and knowing how to manage themselves. Self-esteem comes from knowing that you can do something today that you could not do yesterday, a feeling that school is where learning occurs and the pleasure of knowing what you now know. Establishing these attitudes is so crucial for learning success. Their formation becomes the major focus of the first few weeks of the year.

MANAGING TIME

There are four requirements for which a teacher needs to schedule time. The first is time to experience how readers read, how writers write, how speakers speak, and how we make sense through pictures we see or view and illustrations we create. Through these demonstrations, the teacher talks aloud about how readers, writers, and presenters think. Questions the teacher asks throughout the demonstrations are models for the students of questions they will ask themselves. Demonstrations are part of the everyday routine; they are short, regular, and focused on what is seen as a general learning need (see Chapter 7 for more detailed information on demonstrations).

Second, time must also be set aside to meet with small groups of students with similar needs. Third, time must be spent with individual children to address their specific needs. Fourth, time must be planned to monitor children as they practice new learning and apply learning to new situations (see Chapters 8 and 9 for information on providing instructional support in small groups and to individuals).

An important expectation is that students use their time effectively. They need to know what this means. They need to know that sometimes we meet together as a class, sometimes the teacher will interrupt independent work to call a child into a group, and sometimes during independent work the teacher will be with a particular child.

Over time, students begin to schedule their own literacy work time. This serves two purposes. It enables each student to practice what he or she is learning or has learned. It also develops good work habits, like making independent decisions about what has to be done. Student planning allows a teacher flexibility to work with other groups or individuals while students are independently working. To help establish planning routines and expectations, the first four weeks are critical.

WEEK 1: INTRODUCING THE CLASSROOM

Figure 5.1 shows how time will be used the first week of school.

Grouping	Whole Group		Small Group	Individual	Monitoring
Instructional Approach	Reading Demonstrations	Writing Demonstrations	Small Group	Independent Work	Assessments Collected
Week I	Orientation of book: Front, back, title, author Left to right, return sweep Using pictures to make predictions	Orientation of the draft book page To draw a sketch to convey meaning To orally tell a story from the sketch	Introduce draft book to one group per day My Book assessment	How to: Use classroom materials • Use puzzles in alphabet area and alphabet card • Explore books in classroom library	Observing children while exploring books Observing children in initial draft book writing Observing children with My Book

Figure 5.1: Plan for Week 1

Time in Whole Group

There are a number of things most of these kindergarten students need to know. They need to understand how books work. Demonstrations show them how to identify the front and the back of the book and promote talk about titles and illustrators. Enjoyment is the essential component of reading, but students need to know how one makes sense of what is written. For demonstrations, texts are selected that the children may have heard before and they will want to hear again.

The focus in this first week of demonstrating writing is on how writers sketch to plan. Orientation of the page is important. The plan is at the top and writing beneath. A teacher's demonstration of writing should always be engaging and make sense to five year olds.

Students have a role when teachers work with a whole class. There are expectations about where to sit, how to sit and listen, and what to do as books are read aloud or when the teacher is writing in front of them. Each day those expectations are repeated and explained, and the children's growing attentiveness is acknowledged and praised.

Time in Small Groups

As set out in Figure 5.1, the teacher can bring children in small groups to administer particular pages of the *My Book* assessment. The *My Book* assessment provides a useful opportunity for children to experience short small group time together.

One small group per day is also introduced to writing in a draft book. Preceding this small group introduction, the teacher demonstrates to the whole class what writers do when they write. Children learn from other students as they model what writers do as they write. Through encouragement, the teacher is convincing each student that he or she is a writer regardless of their present stage on the writing continuum.

Being a writer requires constant writing practice. Children will eventually write every day in their draft writing books. Students are taught the orientation of the draft writing book: The top quarter of the page is reserved for the writer's plan, which consists of a pencil sketch of their ideas. This space also has the date. For some children at the beginning of the year the teacher records the date, and for others the teacher provides a model that they can copy. The bottom three quarters of the page is where the students write. Initially the children use a page each day for their writing. A large clip or rubber band can be placed around the draft book to keep the writing pages in sequential order and to discourage young writers from filling every page with writing in the first days of school. Further discussion of writing development is continued in Chapter 8.

Encouraging independence in writing means the teacher avoids sitting alongside children for long periods of time. They must learn to take risks as writers. They need to begin to make choices about topics, draw sketches, and talk about the contents of their plan. They will gain confidence in saying words slowly and writing down the letters they think belong with those sounds. They will begin to read their writing to others and see themselves as writers. Once children have developed positive attitudes about writing, the teacher can develop the knowledge and skills that will move them further along the writing continuum.

Introducing Materials for Independent Work

While the teacher monitors small group writing and administers the *My Book* assessment in small groups, the rest of the children are engaged in other tasks to develop the feeling of independence. The more time spent establishing consistent expectations about working independently at the beginning of the year, the easier the rest of the year becomes.

The early weeks of the year provide opportunities for children to learn how to use materials they will encounter during the remainder of the year and to develop independent work habits. They explore whiteboards and markers, Play-Doh®, Wikki Stix™, puzzles, books, crayons, paper, stickers, stamps, watercolors, and chalkboards, to name a few resources. Exploration of these materials, "playing with them," precedes the use of these materials for instruction or practice. Once the children can work at a few places in the room independently, then the teacher can work for short periods of time with small groups.

Materials are introduced in whole group. Expectations are clearly set out. For example the teacher might ask, "What would we expect it to look like when you are working with the whiteboards and markers?" A list is made about the need to write only on the whiteboard and the need to make certain one can hear the "click" as the lids are replaced on the markers. Photographs are displayed of children using the materials with the expectations listed below. Once the children understand the expectations for using specific materials, the teacher moves between a small group and other children working independently with these materials. Both groups need to experience how it feels to be without the teacher. Individuals need to experience how it feels to be responsible.

Figure 5.2 illustrates the alphabet card. This card is introduced in Week 1. Each student has a card. It is used when a writer is developing sound-to-letter correspondences. (See Chapter 7 for more about the alphabet card.) The teacher has an enlarged alphabet card to use with the whole class.

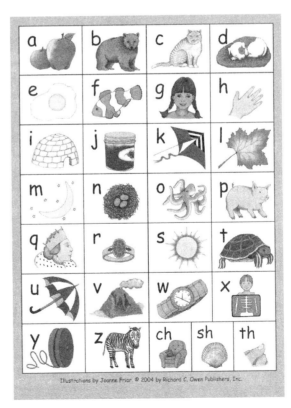

Figure 5.2: The Alphabet Card

Guessing games are played with the alphabet card in the whole group. The children can identify the pictures that can be associated with the letters. The teacher might say, "I am thinking of something you use on a rainy day." UMBRELLA! is the expected response, and the children place a chip to cover the picture. As the children become familiar with the game and variations, it becomes a small group activity for instructional purposes.

Other alphabet games and puzzles are introduced through demonstrations. The class may work together to complete a large floor alphabet puzzle in anticipation of students completing the task independently. The teacher might explain, "When you have finished putting the alphabet puzzle together, it is important to check and make sure you have put the letters in the correct order. Say each letter as you walk on the puzzle to make sure it is all correct."

For children who need instruction on letter identification, the teacher can pull small groups together for practice with materials from the alphabet area of the classroom. When the alphabet area becomes an independent choice, the children have alphabet buddies, so that a child with more letter knowledge is paired with a child who has less letter knowledge. The child who has more experiences with letters provides a model for a child with less experience.

Expectations about the classroom library set the stage for daily reading. In the first week of school, all children read at the same time. They do the same activity. Reading time is preceded each day by a demonstration of reading behavior. The teacher reinforces the expected behaviors. By talking aloud, the teacher can show how readers choose books by looking at the cover and pictures and asking questions such as, "Have I read this book before?" "Is it a book I would like?" "Do the pictures make me ask questions?" "Is there something in the illustrations or photographs that interest me?"

By telling the story through the pictures, teachers demonstrate how readers explore books they cannot yet read. Wordless books are useful for demonstrating how much information one can gain from the pictures as the story is told.

Gathering Assessment Data

Assessment data can be gathered on students' work in whole group and small group, and as the teacher watches or works with individuals. While children are writing, the teacher monitors writing behaviors, looking for the confidence they have as writers and determining if they are beginning to understand what writers do as a result of the demonstrations they have seen. The teacher looks for evidence that even the most emergent writer has the confidence to write strings of letters or lines of scribble. These observations can help to determine if the knowledge of letters and sounds identified from the Observation Survey data are evidenced as the child writes in the draft book. Teachers look for known letters, corresponding sounds, and words. Children are encouraged and praised for their growing confidence. The important thing about becoming a writer is that the students do the writing regardless of their current stage in becoming a writer.

The teacher watches for evidence that students are learning the expectations for working independently. Children are gathered around to watch and listen as other children model these expectations with classroom materials, alphabet games and puzzles, and in the reading area.

While observing children in the book area, the teacher can watch for evidence of book-handling skills with reference to each student's response to the Concepts about Print task discussed in Chapter 4.

These informal observations provide valuable information to the teacher. The teacher's task is to move children on with something they can almost do, but not quite. For that something, students need the teacher's support. The data gathered in the first week of school provides evidence of the nature of support the children need from the teacher in the weeks that follow.

WEEK 2: UNDERSTANDING HOW THE CLASSROOM WORKS

The shift in the use of my time in week two and beyond is based on the students' growing knowledge and confidence in the routines established in the classroom. Figure 5.3 sets out an expanded plan illustrating how time could be used with the whole group, small groups, and as children begin to develop some independence.

Time in Whole Group

The second week of school expands the opportunities for sharing print with children. Nursery rhymes, songs, poetry, finger-plays, jingles, and big books are used. Students will hear these books, songs, poetry, finger-plays, and jingles over and over, and they will learn that the words they hear are associated with the text on the page. This exposure to print builds a repertoire of texts they can revisit. The more familiar they become with these texts, the more children engage in reading them independently.

The teacher can expect students to read a growing list of familiar texts, and they should continue to talk about and practice good classroom habits such as how to use a pointer, appropriate places in the room for reading, how to access the charts and books, and how to put them away. The teacher also talks about how loud our voices should be when we read or sing.

Grouping	Whole Group		Small Group	Individual	Monitoring
Instructional Approach	Reading Demonstrations	Writing Demonstrations	Small Group	Independent Work	Assessments Collected
Week 2	Orientation of book: Front, back, title, author Left to right, return sweep Use pictures to make predictions Use pictures as the text is read Develop a large repertoire of texts	Draw a sketch to plan for writing Orally tell a story from my sketch Use plan to support writing Innovate on familiar texts	Draft book writing in small groups Introduce illustrating to small groups Introduce telling stories using flannel board characters Introduce listening to stories at the listening area	Alphabet games Book exploration How to: Use classroom materials	Observing student reading Observing student writing Observing students in interactions in small groups and with individuals

Figure 5.3: Expanded Plan for Week 2

Along with these shared reading experiences, students learn to innovate on texts shared. Books with a very familiar pattern are read again and again, and once the text is very familiar, then the text can be changed to include references to children in the class. For instance, an innovation on *Mary Wore Her Red Dress and Henry Wore His Green Sneakers* (Peek 1988) becomes a permanent record of what children wore on the first days of school. The teacher can use their drawings as an assessment of their perception of themselves and their understanding of how to use space on the page. Together the drawings become a book children can enjoy again and again. Through this kind of shared activity, the teacher discusses how illustrators think about size, color, and texture in their work. Text innovations become wall displays, with other books on the bookshelves. Children enjoy finding a book with their name and the names of their classmates in it.

Time in Small Groups

Routines introduced and reinforced through demonstrations and shared experiences can be practiced initially as a whole class experience. In this second week, the teacher watches for signs of confidence and independence in order to decide when and which students are ready to take responsibility to work in small groups.

Introducing areas such as the listening post, the illustration space, and the storytelling area can be done more effectively in small groups. During the second week, these tasks are introduced to one group per day while the rest of the class is engaged in other activities. For example, the class is working on tissue paper names (gluing small pieces of squashed tissue paper on a large piece of paper with their name written on it). This becomes a model for instruction to differentiate between upper- and lowercase letters later. While children engage in this work, the listening post can be introduced to another group in the following way.

Four children come with the teacher to the listening post. They learn where to sit and how to find a book and a tape, how to insert the tape in the tape recorder, and how to wear the headsets. Expectations are set for where the book is placed as you listen, how to turn the tape recorder on, what to do when the tape is playing, and when the tape is ended how to return the book and tape to their proper place. The children practice these behaviors.

A similar procedure introduces storytelling. Initially, the only items in the area are a few flannel board stories. The students know the stories. They have been told and retold frequently to the whole group and the children have participated in these retellings. They understand that more than one person can tell the story and manipulate the characters. In the small groups, children learn how the flannel board works, where the stories are stored, and they are reminded how the story can be told by more than one person. The teacher helps organize the first few retellings, explaining that the children can explore this area themselves. The teacher then checks on the rest of the class.

Whole group and small group experiences are part of the daily routine. Children can be expected to work for longer periods of time as the teacher works with individuals and a range of small groups. In Week 2, the responsibility is being placed on the students for their own learning.

Working Independently and Learning About More Options

As children are being introduced to the learning areas of the classroom during the first two weeks of school, they are also introduced to icons that represent these areas (see icons in Appendix E). When introducing children to these areas, the teacher might say, "This is the sign you will see when you explore books."

The next day the children may find the icon on a strip of paper and write their name below it as a "ticket" for exploring books. The next day they may mark a box next to the icon when they have worked in that learning space. All of this is in preparation for the individual planning they will do in Week 3 and beyond.

Gathering Assessment Data

During Week 2, the teacher focuses more specifically on certain behaviors when gathering data. For instance, how many children, after the first week of school, are able to identify the front and the back of the book? Who understands how to orient the page in the draft book? What behaviors change as children explore classroom materials and work in table groups on the same activity? Who can listen to directions and follow them? Who is gaining confidence in asking for help when needed? Who is beginning to understand when it is their time to talk and their time to listen?

WEEK 3: USING THE CLASSROOM, MAKING MORE CHOICES

Figure 5.4 shows the shifts made in Week 3.

Time in Whole Group

Based on the observations made during the first few weeks of school, the teacher can begin to see patterns that are emerging about the whole class of students. These patterns provide the evidence for decision making about whole group instruction. For example, the teacher has observed during the small group work with draft books that many students are unable to tell a story based on their planning sketches in the draft books. Telling a story from a planning sketch becomes the objective for the teacher's daily writing demonstrations. The teacher draws the sketch, then thinks aloud about the story deliberately, putting more detail into the oral description of the story.

Grouping	Whole Group		Small Group	Individual	Monitoring
Instructional Approach	Reading Demonstrations	Writing Demonstrations	Small Group	Independent Work	Assessments Collected
Week 3	Using pictures to make predictions	Drawing a sketch to plan for writing	Draft book writing	Alphabet games	Observing student reading
	Using pictures as the story is read	Orally telling a story from my sketch	Publishing and illustrating	Book exploration	Observing student writing
	Confirming predictions	Using plan to support writing	Introduce handwriting	Listening post	Observing students in interactions in small groups and with individuals
		Using the alphabet card to support writing		Flannel board	
				How to use: Classroom materials	

Figure 5.4: Shifting the Plan for Week 3

Time in Small Groups

The first experience with handwriting instruction occurs in small group. The teacher watches and supports each child in the group. Handwriting instruction begins by using the student's name. A correct model is provided for each child. The first letter of their name is uppercase; the others lowercase. The teacher can demonstrate with his or her own name. It is important to closely watch the children practice writing their names, observing their level of confidence, their control of letter formation, and their control of space.

Draft book writing continues in small groups; the children who have written the previous day will illustrate those books in a small group the following day.

Making Choices for Independent Work

By Week 3, the children are ready to use individual planning sheets. The teacher decides what the children will do and when they will do it. An initial planning sheet may look like the one set out in Figure 5.5. (See Appendix F for templates.)

There are two parts to a planning sheet. Items that are on the top of the plan are activities the child must engage in daily (reading and writing at the beginning of the year). Children decide what they will do first and second. Once they decide the order for the "must do" tasks, they plan others and set them out below the line. These activities will support and extend literacy learning: alphabet area, listening area, storytelling, and so on. As they complete these tasks, they cross them off.

name: _____ date: / /

Monday   Tuesday   Wednesday   Thursday   Friday

reading	writing
alphabet	poetry
listening	spelling
investigation	storytelling

Figure 5.5: Sample Plan for Beginning of Year

Over the year, some tasks will remain the same while others will be replaced as children develop additional skills. For instance, the alphabet area will not be needed once children are able to identify the letters in the alphabet. It will be replaced with opportunities for children to work with words (Pinnell and Fountas 2002).

As children begin to understand the expectations and the need to comply with the requirements of time and behavior, greater responsibility for planning is turned over to them. Some learners will need more support than others in how their time is used. The teacher meets with small groups of children each day to support their choices for planning or even decide the plan for those not yet ready to plan on their own. The goal is for all students to make responsible planning decisions for their independent learning.

Gathering Data

In Week 3, data gathering becomes more specific as students become more engaged in small group and individual work. Information about student handwriting can be gathered daily from observing the children as they practice. Looking at the size of the writing, their knowledge of letters, and how efficiently they make the letter forms provides valuable assessment data as set out in Figure 5.6.

I note that Quenton:
- Can write his name
- Accurately forms *U, o*
- Uses uppercase letter at beginning
- Uses lowercase for other letters
- Approximates *e, t, n*
- Next step: Where to start with *e, t*
- Formation of *n*

Figure 5.6: Assessment Data on Handwriting

The teacher can observe the impact of demonstrations on the students in the classroom. Based on the focused demonstrations about oral rehearsal for a writing story, which students are better able to tell their own stories? Is there a difference in how children are retelling known stories with flannel board characters? What do children say as they as they look at book illustrations?

WEEK 4: MANAGING TIME AND LEARNING

Time in Whole Group

Whole group instruction continues to be focused on the broad patterns revealed from the assessment data collected. The teacher looks for opportunities to make an impact on most students through these daily demonstrations.

Demonstrations become more focused in both reading and writing. The teacher uses pictures to both predict and confirm the story content when reading. Emphasis is placed on making certain the student plan supports the oral rehearsal, which guides the writing of the piece.

Time in Small Groups

In Week 4, the teacher has gathered sufficient information to bring together groups with similar needs. Initially small group instruction is helping children understanding how to operate in these small groups. Talk focuses on how to come to the floor or reading table, how to stay on the same page as our classmates and the teacher when we're reading, and on how to hold the book and turn the pages. Students practice taking turns talking about the pictures and looking at the person who is doing the talking, while actively listening to what that person is saying. This continues the development of work habits that will lead to effective group work throughout the year.

Developing Independence

Initial data collected about the children is being confirmed through observations during the first weeks of school. Most students are emergent readers. The best reading materials for students to practice new reading skills are books that are easy for them to read. Easy texts help readers develop fluency and phrasing. Oral reading records show which texts these children can read at 97–100% accuracy. According to the oral reading record, once a child's reading level has been established, appropriate books for independent reading are collected and placed in an independent book box or bag for each student.

At the beginning of the year many of the independent reading books are the students' own published books, wordless books, and a few trade books. As competence and confidence in reading grow, the number of trade books increases.

MONITORING THE TEACHER'S EFFECTIVENESS IN MANAGING LEARNING

A teacher's own effectiveness can be measured by the precision and focus brought to instruction. The effectiveness of instruction is found in what students learn.

Since learning only occurs when students are engaged, another measure of my instructional effectiveness is the level of engagement that students show in literacy tasks. Engagement occurs when learners are challenged, but not frustrated with the tasks they are assigned. They are interested because the task is meaningful, and only become frustrated or bored because the task is tedious. Teachers can identify engagement through the intensity of children's involvement.

If the teacher is constantly calling students to task, continually interrupting to quiet them, always admonishing because of minor scuffles rather than managing their learning, it is time for reassessment.

- What learning is occurring for this child?
- Is the task too difficult or too easy?
- Do the materials challenge or frustrate?
- Is there sufficient variation?
- Are the students confronted with not enough to do or with too many choices?

Periodically, teachers should take time to stand back and observe: watching children with tasks they've been assigned, with materials they are manipulating, as they are interacting with other adults and with each other. What changes could be made to improve learning and learning opportunities? Constant assessment and reassessment of a teacher's work ensures instruction is accurately matching children to the work they engage in.

This chapter has explored an organization of learning experiences that might be put into place the first few weeks of school. It is less daunting when teachers are clear about what they expect students to be able to do and how systematically they approach the task of supporting students doing it.

Organizing and managing student learning has much to do with common sense and what is known about effective and exemplary teaching (Morrow, Tracey, Woo, & Pressley 1999; Pressley, Rankin, & Yokoi 1996; Ruddell & Ruddell 1995). A summary of these researchers would characterize effective instructional environments as having:

- A rich literacy environment with accessible materials
- The careful organization and management of strategies and structures for optimal literacy development to occur
- Varied structures for instruction, including whole group, small group, and individual settings with the teacher
- Instruction adjusted to meet the individual needs of students
- Opportunities for children to work independently of the teacher, either alone or in social cooperative groups
- Opportunities for children to practice the skills learned
- High expectations for student accomplishment
- An environment where children are treated with respect.

The physical organization of space and materials is important. The design of areas for learning, and the expectations and management of how learners use time is crucial to effective learning.

Searching for new ways to keep children busy, new behavior management systems, and new strategies for instruction is unlikely to address classroom organizational and management issues that are not well thought through in the first place. Time spent organizing the environment and providing clear demonstrations of the use of materials to manage learning will foster engagement, engender responsibility, and lead to successful learning.

Effective teachers know what their learners know, and effective teachers know what their students need to learn next and can organize an environment that helps manage their students' learning. Teachers can decide how to plan their time and meet each of the student's needs. One thing known for sure is that teachers are the best predictors of student learning success.

6   planning my time to manage student learning

Teachers need to be comfortable with the way the classroom environment is organized. As suggested in the previous chapter, they need routines and procedures in place to manage the learning of the diverse range of students. Several weeks into the school year, routines are established and students know what to do when they are working with the teacher. They know what to do when they plan to work independently.

The four sections of this chapter are about teacher planning: how planning is managed for the year ahead, how planning is done month by month, how weeks in the month are planned, and how the weekly plan breaks down to daily work. The rationale for this planning is as follows:

- Yearly planning addresses content expectations of district and state standards; it provides the focus for what we are learning and how well we have learned it
- Monthly planning is about meeting the needs identified from the patterns found in my assessment data
- Weekly planning is based on the amount and frequency of instruction that arise from different rates of learning growth
- Daily planning is about meeting learning needs today based on the students' strengths and gaps that I observed yesterday.

Planning is the allocation of time. It is a schedule of what is done on a daily, weekly, monthly, and yearly basis. The daily schedule is an action plan. It sets out what happens with the whole class together, with small groups, or with individuals and their understandings, knowledge, and literacy skills. The way this learning is managed for each student is included in the schedule of whole group, small group, and individual time.

YEARLY PLANNING

The kindergarten curriculum is typically set out as content proficiencies to be achieved rather than particular content to be covered. The content standards in most states are first assessed by standardized testing in grade three. Since the content standards are on a continuum of learning, kindergarten teachers have a responsibility to ensure that the standards expected of their students are met or exceeded. The literacy standards for kindergarten students begin the formal continuum for literacy learning through the grades.

Content Standards

The kindergarten content standards in reading and writing will vary from state to state and district to district, but they are not inconsistent with the broad literacy expectations set out in this book. There are also content standards in the other subjects such as social studies and science. Children come to school with a range of knowledge about the content of these subjects, just as they do with a range of skills in literacy. Many have yet to develop the vocabulary and language needed to understand concepts in science or social studies. To learn the content, they need literacy skills, but science and social studies are not additional to reading and writing; they are part of reading and writing. The following links to literacy when planning for social studies and science provide examples.

Social Studies

Teachers are responsible for planning content topics across the school year. The social studies curriculum sets out the content that is expected to be learned. For the first month of school, this content easily becomes the content of reading and writing as well. For example, if students are expected to develop the social skills involved in working as a classroom group, they learn that as part of developing good work and study habits, learning how to participate in whole group and small group, and how to engage in individual work. They are expected to be assuming responsibility and making their own decisions. They are asked to work together, which requires solving problems independently. The social studies curriculum is part of what is expected to be happening in a reading and writing classroom.

Science

A science curriculum can be handled the same way as social studies. Teachers usually begin the kindergarten year with the study of self: Students are expected to describe their physical characteristics, understand how the five senses work, label the parts of the body, and articulate how to care for it. Five year olds are egocentric. They bring all kinds of experiences about themselves to school. These experiences can be shared through writing, speaking, and presenting. The science curriculum provides the topics for children to read, write, and talk about what they know best—themselves!

Figure 6.1 sets out typical units in science and social studies for the first two months of school, based upon the planning described above.

Months of School	Science Content	Social Studies Content
Month 1 My Classroom • Who am I? • What do I do? • Who are my friends? • How are we the same? • How are we different?	Study of Self • Physical Characteristics • Five Senses	Citizenship • Participation • Decision Making • Problem Solving • Responsibility
Month 2 My Family • Who am I? • Who is in my family? • What do I do? • How are we the same as other families? • How are we different?	Study of Self • Parts of body • Care of body	Families • Description of own family • Comparisons to families of other students • Roles

Figure 6.1: Planning for Content Areas in the First Two Months
of School

The content becomes topics for demonstrations and opportunities to work in small groups and independently. Instruction is driven by the learner's need; the content becomes a vehicle. Teachers demonstrate how readers read and how writers write, and they think about the interests of five year olds in order to select books that have relevant content yet develop reading and writing skills. They demonstrate topics that foster engagement, such as their own experiences as a child, experiences their own children have had, places they have been with their children, and people in their immediate and extended family. The working spaces of the room can include the content focus for the first two months of school.

The yearly plan also provides one framework for exposing children to content language they may not have. It brings intention to the development of oral language. For instance, when the content is pets and animal care, the children experience and talk about collars, leashes, dog dishes and food, bird cages and seed, and pet toys. They can listen to stories about tabby cats, parakeets, and dogs following an ice cream truck. Stories can become the background. They access them and use reading, writing, listening, speaking, viewing, and presenting to broaden their knowledge and skills in both content and the media through which they learn it.

MONTHLY PLANNING

Figure 6.2 sets out a sample monthly plan for October and November, which can be kept on a clipboard with the weekly and daily plan. Monthly planning tests the effectiveness of the classroom instruction. The data collected about each child in the past four weeks is reviewed and the teacher asks two kinds of questions.

The first concerns attitudes toward literacy:

- To what extent do my students see themselves as readers and writers?

The second question concerns knowledge and skills:

- What can my students do now? What evidence do I have about what they know and can do?

Developing Attitudes in Writing

After a month in school, teachers will develop expectations about their students as readers and writers; they can see their students gaining confidence and developing positive attitudes. The evidence is found in observing students. While not every child is at the same level of proficiency, most of them should be:

- Choosing topics for their writing
- Writing about things that are important to them (knowing the ABC's, going to visit grandma or cousins, getting new slippers)
- Beginning to know writing is supposed to make sense
- Reading their published books independently
- Adding some details to their sketch for planning
- Using pictures as a source of information when reading published books to predict or confirm content

Literacy Planning for Month of: <u>October 18 – November 18</u> # MONTHLY PLAN

READING/WRITING DEMONSTRATIONS

OUTCOME: To ask questions of myself as I read and write to ensure meaning is paramount.	
READERS	WRITERS
What might this book be about? What do I think will happen next? Does that make sense in the story? How can I use the pictures to help me? What letter do I expect to see? Is that the word ____? What words did the writer use to give me a picture in my head? What would I do if I were writing this book?	What will I write? What needs to be in my plan? Do I have enough information in my plan? How will I begin this piece? What will make it sound interesting? What sounds do I hear in the word I need to write? What letter makes that sound? How do I write the word ____? Does my writing make sense? Who will want to read it?

SMALL GROUPS

INSTRUCTIONAL OBJECTIVE	GROUP
Word-by-word matching	1 Alberto, Sophie, Dani, Celeste, Julio, Jaren
Directionality (focus-return sweep)	2 Celia, Kyle, Jasmine, Quenton
Attending closely to print to anticipate & confirm	3 Anna, Paul, Colin, Jazz, Marcy
Word-by-word matching	4 Charles, Maria, Keisha
Monitoring by checking meaning & visual	5 Nina, José
Eyes on print, where to start, L to R	6 Janisha, Caleb

INDIVIDUAL SKILLS/MONITORING LEARNING

3x OR MORE SKILL INSTRUCTION		DAILY INSTRUCTION	
STUDENTS	SKILLS	STUDENTS	SKILLS
Dani	Letter ID	Celia	Where to start
Celeste	Sound to letter	Kyle	Directionality
Julio	Beg. sounds	Jasmine	Letter ID
Jaren	Ending sounds	Quenton	Letter formation
Anna	Spaces btw. words	Janisha	Sound to letter
Paul	Phonetic generalizations	Caleb	High frequency words
Colin	Clusters of sounds	Charles	
Jazz	High frequency words	Maria	
Marcy	Spelling approximations	Keisha	
Nina	Handwriting	Alberto	
José		Sophie	
Beau			

MONITORING INDIVIDUAL APPLICATION

* Engagement in poetry, charts, songs
* Engagement in independent reading and writing
* Story structure in storytelling, book language

Figure 6.2: Sample Monthly Planning Sheet

- Answering questions about their reading and writing
- Matching the writing to their plan
- Identifying the front and back of books (whether on their own published book or a trade book)
- Identifying the title of the book
- Knowing where to begin when reading and writing.

My Own Classroom as I Develop a Monthly Plan

The notes that I have made and the samples I have gathered about each student are represented by the examples in Figures 6.3 through 6.5 showing what Celia, Julio, and Nina can now do. Compare these latest notes with those I made in Chapter 2 when these children entered kindergarten. Compare, also, the samples of their work. This kind of evidence supports their learning growth in writing. They each believe they are now writers. I know they are writers.

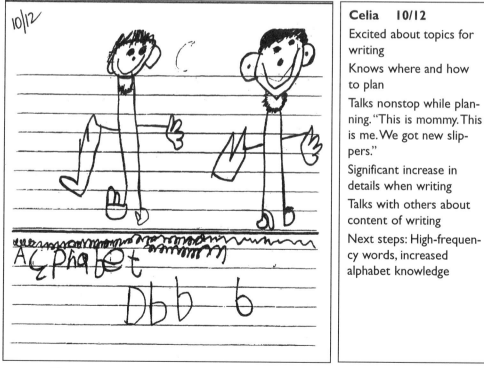

Celia 10/12

Excited about topics for writing

Knows where and how to plan

Talks nonstop while planning. "This is mommy. This is me. We got new slippers."

Significant increase in details when writing

Talks with others about content of writing

Next steps: High-frequency words, increased alphabet knowledge

Figure 6.3: I have Barney slippers. Mommy has bunny slippers.

Julio   10/7

Knows where to plan where to write

Adds details to sketch and talks about topic

Uses initial sounds consistently and beginning to use ending sounds

Directionality firmly in place

Essential words— *I, to,* approx. *the*

Next steps: Spaces between words, high-frequency words, consolidate ending sounds, middle sounds

Figure 6.4: I went to the park.

Nina   10/14

Determines her topic before she comes to school

Details to sketch reveal a level of sophistication (speech balloon—HEY!, angry facial expression)

More oral language to her story than what is written down.

Increased consistency in lowercase letters (*y, o, t, s, a*)

Spelling approximation (*hores—horse*) using visual information

Added 10 words to known essential words.

Next steps: Adding onto writing, lowercase letters, essential words, spelling: close approximations

Figure 6.5: My horse got in a horse fight.

Developing Attitudes in Reading

Attitudes are as equally important in the developing reader as they are in the developing writers. I want my students to see themselves as readers. The classroom library is "the place to be" when children are working independently. There has been a real shift in how they engage with books. Children who came to school knowing very few books now have a larger repertoire of familiar stories and books. I see them lie on their stomachs with books, sit with them in their laps, and hold them up for an audience when they are "playing at reading." Our book innovations such as *Mary Wore Her Red Dress* (discussed in Chapter 5) have been bound into big books. They are taken off the walls, read on the floor, and have become great favorites. The nursery rhymes we recite daily are on charts and are consistent choices for independent reading.

Folktales such as "The Three Little Pigs," "Billy Goats Gruff," and "The Three Bears" are collected together in one area of the classroom library. More than one version of each is available. As I rove in this space, I hear the use of book language as these stories are told and retold. My notes suggest that most children are:

- Selecting books that interest and sustain them for longer periods of time
- Beginning to know that reading is supposed to make sense
- Returning to favorite books frequently
- Reading their published books independently at their current stage of development
- Using pictures as a source of information to predict or confirm content when reading published books
- Using pictures as a source of information when playing at reading, and exploring books to predict content and retell the story
- Asking questions and talking about the book they are reading
- Identifying the front and back of books (whether their own published book or a trade book)
- Knowing where to begin when reading and writing.

Happily, children who came to school confident in their ability to read and write have maintained this confidence. Others have gained in confidence.

Effective teacher demonstrations develop good attitudes. They show what readers and writers do: the questions we ask ourselves as readers and writers, and the way we respond in our reading and writing. Demonstrations show how we make sense of our reading and writing by asking questions as we read and write. In the Monthly Plan (see Figure 6.2) I have set out the questions I ask aloud in my demonstrations during the second month of kindergarten.

Developing Knowledge and Skills

I am expecting my students will show confidence in using their literacy skills. With confidence comes independence, and that grows with an increase in knowledge and skills. Figures 6.6 through 6.8 show the evidence I have gathered about the literacy growth of Celia, Julio, and Nina in the first two months of school and what I have noted about their growth in competence as readers.

Looking at similar evidence across the whole class, I can see how the others have developed also. Some will have progressed quickly, others more slowly. Patterns begin to emerge. I see the need to review my small groups.

Celia   10/11

Increased engagement in reading area of classroom

Identifies front and back of book without support

Retells familiar stories in storytelling area (Three Bears, Three Little Pigs)

"Plays at reading," holding book like teacher

Identifies letters of name in context and in alphabet games

Knows where to start when reading

Is beginning to identify known letters in texts

Attending to pictures in library and listening area

Talking about pictures with others

Returns to same books in library and rereads with growing expression

Reads word—*I*

Oral Reading Record: Slippers (own published book) (See Literacy Record)

Summary Statement: Knows front and back of book, knows where to start. Controls L to R, gaining control of return sweep

Next Steps: Consolidate return sweep with directionality; word-by-word matching

---

Figure 6.6: Evidence of Celia's Literacy Learning

Celia			
Date	SP TB	Record of Oral Reading	Summary Statement
9|6	TB	Title: I Can Read	Uses pictures as a source of information. Invents text based on pictures. Turns pages Next step - Where to start, LtoR
10|2	SP	Title: Slippers Text: I have Barney slippers. Mommy has Bunny slippers. ✓ ✓ now ✓ ✓ and they are purple. ✓ ✓ new ✓ ✓ and they are pink.	Knows front and back of book. Knows where to start. Controls LtoR, gaining control of Return sweep NS — Return sweep - word-by word matching

Key: SP - Student Published; TB - Trade Book

Figure 6.6: Evidence of Celia's Literacy Learning (continued)

Julio 10/12

Chooses to explore books from read-alouds, often asks to take them home

Directionality firmly in place

Chooses to read published books daily and share with peers

Closer approximations with word-by-word matching

Looks for known words when reading

Searches pictures for more information—"He's in trouble now, look at his Mom's face"

Uses pointer to approximate word-by-word matching on poetry charts

Can identify *h, n, m, w, r, f*

Attends to initial letters "Hey they made a mistake. It's supposed to be a *b* and they put an *s*!" Text: story Child: book

Watches others in storytelling area, occasionally goes there alone.

Oral reading record: My Clubhouse (own published book) (See Literacy Record)

Summary Statement: Left to right, return sweep. Reread when voice did not match text; self-corrected for visual/meaning

Next steps: Attend to the visual source of information (initial letter): look past 1st letter to predict unknown word

Figure 6.7: Evidence of Julio's Literacy Learning

Nina

Asks to take books home to read to sister

No longer confused with first/last (can identify page, word in sentence, letter in word)

Used book language when dramatizing Three Pigs—"not by the hair of my..."

Willing to read to others in the reading area

Engages for long periods of time in reading area reading both trade books and published books

Consistently used first letter at difficulty

Interested in exploring informational texts

Oral reading record: Cat Tails (E2) 90% accuracy (See Literacy Record)

Summary Statement: Consistently used meaning and structure. Attended to first letter but meaning and structure override when she can't substitute a word that looks right.

Next Steps: Look past 1st letter to predict unknown words (blends)

Figure 6.8: Evidence of Nina's Literacy Learning

Flexibility

Children move in and out of groups, and new groups are formed over the month, depending on the learning that occurs as a result of my instruction. Groups have to be flexible. A key to successfully using groups is flexibility. The composition of the word-by-word matching groups is changed because some children have learned the skill more rapidly and are beginning to apply it independently. Some children are moved to another group that I will meet with three times during the next week. The remaining children are still learning the skill. They need more practice as they read. The lowest performing children on this skill sit close to me so I can guide their fingers as they read. When I see the application of new learning, for instance, seeing word-by-word matching during independent reading and on poetry charts, I can reduce the frequency of small group instruction for this objective.

Individual Students

Teachers continue to work with individual students, particularly those emergent writers whose writing is published daily. (This is discussed further in Chapter 9.) This one-on-one instruction is focused on one or two teaching points from the students' writing. The emphasis at this stage is getting it down on paper, directionality, letter identification, sounds-to-letter relationship, letter formation, and the learning of high frequency words. These published books support the development of reading skills because they are also the child's first reading material. However, it is impossible to meet with all students one-on-one, so it is appropriate to plan small groups for instruction around similar objectives.

Consolidation of Behaviors to Foster Independent Learning

Reviewing the level of monthly progress informs the teacher about the instruction that has been provided, the effectiveness of that instruction, and what behaviors to observe as new learning. The teacher knows what to look for and where to find the application of that learning.

- Is directionality being learned by the reader and being used by the writer?
- In the classroom library, does the student use pictures as a source of information as they do when illustrating their published books?
- When reading poetry are students using word-by-word matching?
- Do they have a sense of story as they work in the storytelling area?

These kinds of questions prompt the systematic observation that confirms the effectiveness of my instruction and informs my monthly plan.

WEEKLY PLANNING

Traditional weekly teaching plans consisted of the topics to be covered set out by days and time schedules. Teaching began on Monday morning and was expected to end on Friday afternoon. Often by Tuesday or Wednesday these traditional plans had little relevance as a guide to instruction. By then, some children were so far ahead and some so far behind that teachers were unable to address their range of learning needs. Changes had to be made if student learning needs were to be met. In one sense, the shift was made from teaching the kindergarten curriculum to teaching children. When children are the focus, their learning needs become the guide to instruction. Weekly planning now is based upon what is learned daily about the needs of the students.

Weekly planning begins with a review of the past week. The daily plans prompt some simple questions.

- What learning is a result of whole group instruction or demonstrations?
- What about the success of small group instruction?
- What about the individuals with whom the teacher has worked?
- What shifts should be made within the daily schedule to use the teacher's time more effectively?

My Own Time as I Develop a Weekly Plan

Figure 6.9 sets out my weekly plan. From this plan, decisions are made about teaching objectives. Teachers look for evidence of learning as a result of their instruction. Decisions are made about narrowing the focus or accelerating instruction. For example, I have been working daily with a small group to use the picture as a source of information for predicting the storyline. Because the students are beginning to attend more closely to the text, I observe that they now dive right into the text and ignore the picture. They have made growth because of the instruction that has occurred. Thinking about this, I revise the objective; I will have them check the picture after they have read to confirm the storyline.

The weekly plan keeps the teacher on track ensuring that children are being taught what they need to know, not what they already know. Note in the weekly plan in Figure 6.9 that the six groups have been formed around learning objectives. I keep the group size between three and five children, even though ten children require instruction in word-by-word matching. My instruction will be more effective with five children at a time, so I divide the group. Managing how children will learn is as important as what they need to know.

Daily Publishing

There are eight emergent writers listed on my weekly plan with whom I intend to work one-on-one each day. On my plan, "Daily Publishing" refers to the writing instruction for those children who are still at the emergent stage. These children may not have directionality when writing, have little or no sound-symbol correspondence, and may not have the oral language to plan their writing or describe the plan. Because the skills being developed are skills they are ready for, the frequency and intensity of this instruction in daily writing and publication accelerate their learning. Part of this support is developing independence. The more skills they gain the more independent they are as writers.

Focused Monitoring

Focused instruction is the result of observing specific skills as they are developing. The Literacy Record (see Chapter 4) guides my observation. Each week, I make decisions about what I need to observe with each student. When making my monitoring list, I ask this question, "Who will I be observing, and what am I looking for?"

If I am looking for evidence in both the storytelling area and the classroom library for the individual child's understanding of how stories are organized, I am looking for the application of their knowledge of beginning, middle, and end as they dramatize or tell familiar stories. I listen for book language and story words, particularly characters at this point in the year because the idea of story characters has been emphasized in reading and writing demonstrations.

WEEKLY PLAN

Week of: Oct. 4-8	MONDAY	TUESDAY	WEDNESDAY	THURSDAY	FRIDAY
SMALL GROUP INSTRUCTION Group Numbers	Group 1 Group 2 Group 4 Group 6	Group 1 Group 3 Group 4 Group 5	Group 1 Group 2 Group 4 Group 5	Group 1 Group 3 Group 4 Group 6	Group 1 Group 2 Group 4
DAILY PUBLISHING	Celia Jasmine Jaren Quenton Maria Kyle Janisha Caleb				→
FOCUSED MONITORING Outcome: Story structure	Celia José Quenton Colin Sophie	Julio Dani Jasmine Janisha Kyle	Nina Celeste Beau Marcy Charles	Anna Caleb Jaren Maria Paul	Keisha Jazz Alberto
SPELLING	Nina Alberto	José Keisha	Anna Jazz	Colin Julio	Paul
ORAL READING RECORDS		Paul Jaren Celia	Colin Maria Jasmine	Dani Beau	

GROUP	STUDENT NAMES	INSTRUCTIONAL OBJECTIVE
1	Alberto, Marcy, Keisha, Jazz, Julio	Word-by-word matching
2	Celia, Maria, Jaren, Kyle	Directionality reading/writing
3	Anna, Colin, Paul	Using pictures to confirm Using sketch to plan
4	Sophie, Dani, Beau, Charles, Celeste	Word-by-word matching
5	Nina, José	Monitoring self-correction using visual information/Adding on to writing
6	Janisha, Caleb, Jasmine, Quenton	Eyes on print, Directionality Letter ID

Figure 6.9: Model of a Weekly Plan

Individual Instruction

Note the children selected for daily spelling instruction. These children are closely approximating words in their writing and have a growing list of essential words. (For more specific information on spelling instruction, see Chapters 9 and 10.) Grouping for spelling instruction this way allows me to organize instruction systematically and to meet with each child once a week to introduce the spelling words he or she will be learning.

Oral Reading Records

Systematic monitoring means having an oral reading record no older than three weeks on each child. Because my reading instruction is based on the needs and progress of the individual, I expect that I will see evidence of new learning with each record I take. I can comfortably manage two or three oral reading assessments each day, and I note the students I will work with on my plan. I can refer to my weekly plan, which is attached to my clipboard, each day during the following week.

DAILY PLANNING

The daily plan is like the road map for the day's instruction. This plan is not based on what the teacher *assumes* should happen; it's based on what the teacher knows should happen. The routine of the day is always the same: focusing instruction with a whole group, working with small groups with similar needs, and individual instruction to meet particular needs.

At the end of the previous week, the teacher has recorded information for the following week's daily planning including:

- Groups that will be met with each day, the objective and resource used with that group
- Names of individual students who will be published daily and the focus of their individual instruction
- Objective that will be monitored when children are working independently
- Names of individual students and the day they will receive spelling instruction
- Names of individual students and the day they will receive an oral reading record.

The teacher will delete, revise, and fine-tune each day's plan, based upon the student's responses to instruction and how time has been used.

My Own Classroom as I Develop a Daily Plan

The demonstrations of reading and writing will fit what was learned from student responses yesterday and will be recorded daily. The objective for small group instruction is based on the cluster of similar needs found from analysis of assessment data. Individual learning is planned where more intense one-on-one support is needed. I will meet with individuals for instruction as I publish their writing. I also meet with individuals for spelling instruction, and I schedule time for monitoring the learning of the other individuals I have listed. There is space to record observations and other notes.

Figure 6.10 illustrates a beginning-of-the-year daily planning sheet. It is attached to the clipboard I use throughout the day. It is a dated record of daily instruction. Note that I expect to have an objective or focus and appropriate resources or other tools for each instructional component. Knowing what to do can help the teacher prepare for doing it. Having most of the daily plan recorded at the beginning of the week allows me to plan what will occur during the instructional episodes.

Planning for Instructional Episodes

Teaching objectives come from my most recently evaluated assessment data. This informs me of what the children need to learn. Note as one example of daily planning I will meet with Alberto, Jazz, Keisha, Julio, and Marcy for small group instruction to develop the skill of word-by-word matching.

My assessment data shows me that these five students know that reading and writing begins at the left side of the page and goes to the right with a return sweep. I note each of them is approximating at word-by-word matching. My objective is to develop this skill.

I begin with what I know. Each child can use what they hear (aural language), what they say (oral language), what they see (viewing) to support meaning making, and they are beginning to make sense of what they read. Figure 6.11 (page 125) illustrates sample pages from the book *Bedtime* (Finney 2001). I use this information as I select the text for instruction.

The setting and characters in *Bedtime* are familiar to children: a child's room, family members, a special blanket, and a teddy bear. The theme is one that they understand and have experienced: avoiding bedtime. The pictures in the book provide more information than the words on the page. The print is large and the spaces between the words and below the line of print support word-by-word matching. There is a pattern to some of the text so the children know what to

Literacy Planning for Date: _Oct. 5_

DAILY PLAN

WRITING DEMONSTRATION
Obj: To match writing with planning sketch

Topic: Burnt Toast

READING DEMONSTRATION
Obj: To use pictures to anticipate.

Text: I Went Walking (Sue Williams)

SONGS/POETRY
If you're Happy and you Know It

Head, Shoulders, Knees, Toes

Down By the Station

Small Group Instruction

READING
Obj: Word-by word matching
Group: Alberto, Keisha, Jazz, Julio, Marcy
Resource: So Sleepy

READING
Obj: Directionality (L to R)
Group: Celia, Jaren, Kyle, Maria
Resource: The Pond

WRITING
Obj: Using plan to tell story
Group: Anna, Paul, Colin
Resource: Draft Book

ALPHABET
Obj: Match pictures to letters
Group: Janisha, Caleb, Beau, Jasmine, Quenton
Resource:

Publishing

NAME	TEACHING POINT
*Celia	→ add to plan
*Jaren	→ L to R
*Maria	→ talk about plan
*Kyle	→ plan matches story
*Janisha	→ plan matches story
*Caleb	→ plan matches story
*Jasmine	→ oral language / L to R
*Quenton	→ L to R
Jazz	→ use of "t", word "my"
Keisha	→ ending sounds
Celeste	→ end sounds
*Daily Sophie	→ reinforce "I"

Spelling
José
Keisha

Oral Reading
Paul
Jaren
Celia

Monitoring Learning
Focus: Story structure - classroom library puppets
Who? Julio, Dani, Jasmine, Janisha, Kyle

NOTES

Figure 6.10: Teacher's Daily Plan

It is bedtime.

I need my blanket.

**Figure 6.11: Sample Pages
from *Bedtime***

anticipate. The text contains familiar words that are anchors for these children such as *I, a, my,* and *is*. The book has one line of text per page but within that line of text there are subtle changes. Most pages begin with the pattern, "I need my..." and there are both one word and two words at the end of that pattern ("I need my pillow." "I need my teddy bear.") These are useful challenges for the children. Other challenges occur at the end of the book, when the pattern changes once again: "I need a story, please."

I want the children to make links between their own bedtime experiences and the experiences of the child in the book. We will talk about what they do before they go to bed, such as getting a drink, reading a story, brushing teeth, and finding a favorite soft toy. I can write these things on a chart so they can use their ideas and confirm them through the text. We will talk about what they expect to find out when reading this book.

I look for places in the text where I will monitor individual children's progress with word-by-word matching. I will be looking for repeated pattern of text to see if there is any indication that confidence is increasing. I will also watch for self-corrections when the word being pointed to does not match a known word.

All instruction requires the same type of thinking. I decide from my assessment data about the number of children who will be grouped. I decide the teaching objective. I identify what will tell me the children are learning. I select resources or learning experiences that offer support to the students by building on what they currently know.

FROM YEARLY PLANNING TO DAILY PLANNING— MANAGING STUDENT LEARNING

The yearly plan is a guide. It helps to deliver the content of science and social studies. The yearly plan also provides a framework for demonstrations, shared experiences, and the learning spaces in the classroom. The plan helps expand the content curriculum from a focus on self and family to a world beyond.

Monthly planning is the opportunity to reflect on the effectiveness of the instruction. It results from a systematic look at individual learning. It helps reveal patterns of learning and allows the teacher to set longer-term targets for instruction.

Planning for the week ahead enables the teacher to fine-tune instructional objectives and to group and regroup flexibly. The amount of support individuals and groups need during that week suggest how time is allocated each day. It provides the skeletal framework for the daily plan.

My daily plan is specific. It is an action plan. It sets out the time schedule for the day and how the student's time will be allocated to whole group work, small group instruction, and independent work. It can also set out the resources needed and other preparation for the day. The daily plan is what the teacher does today, based on what was learned yesterday.

Teaching is providing the necessary amount of support for new learning to occur: bringing the learner, the teacher, and the learning experience together to close the gap between what the learner can do and what the learner is ready to do.

7 the child is the guide to instruction

Creating learning success for children in kindergarten means every moment of the kindergarten day should be a learning moment. Learning is closing the gap between what the child can do and what the child needs to do next. Anticipating what a child is ready to learn is one of the teacher's most important jobs since this identifies what they are not yet able to do and where they need support.

Children who create an approximation of the word *dog* (for example, spelled *dg*) are writing what they hear. This close attempt deserves just the right amount of instruction to get it right. The addition of one letter to correct the spelling is something the child is ready and able to do with the teacher's support, but something the child would be unlikely to do alone. Instruction in this sense moves ahead of the child and anticipates a readiness to learn.

As Lev Vygotsky, a Russian psychologist who studied the behaviors of children learning language, commented, "The only good kind of instruction is that which marches ahead of development and leads it; it must be aimed not so much at the ripe as at the ripening function... Instruction must be oriented at the future, not the past" (Vygotsky 1978). This concept runs counter to many kindergarten teaching practices. For example, teaching every alphabet letter and sound to the whole class ignores what most teachers know: Many children entering kindergarten have some alphabet knowledge. The daily rote and repetition of alphabet instruction for these students becomes tedious and downright boring. Negative attitudes to learning can be seeded very easily.

Observing children as they engage in literacy—and recording what they say and do—can identify what the child already knows. The gap between what they know and what they need to learn next is "the zone of proximal development...the distance between the child's current individual capacity and the capacity to perform with assistance" (Vygotsky 1978, 188). What the child needs to do next exposes the "ripening function." The judgment that teachers bring to decisions about what students need to learn is what distinguishes them as professionals.

Professional decisions determine the instructional approaches and materials that will be used to close the gap between what the student knows and what he or she needs to know. This idea is very different from relying on recipes, programs, or teaching methodologies that focus on what is being taught. When the focus is on instruction, one cannot lose sight of the child. Thinking moves from, "What should I teach today?" to "What should this child be learning today?"

Vygotsky also argues that a child's development is influenced by the "external social world in which that individual's life has developed" (Tharp and Gallimore 1993, 7). Learning occurs best in a social context, with the support of a more experienced other. The kindergarten classroom becomes the social context for learning and a real-life world where children represent their thoughts through authentic literacy experiences. As noted earlier, kindergarten is not just a preparation for life; *it is real life* for the five year old. Classroom literacy experiences need to be meaningful and purposeful. Students need to see purpose in what they are doing. They need to know that what they write about will be read by someone interested in what they are writing, and that what they read is interesting, engaging, and makes sense to a five year old.

AUTHENTIC LEARNING ENVIRONMENTS

The social nature of the classroom provides at least two important characteristics of an authentic learning environment. Both Holdaway (1979) and Cambourne (1988) identified a series of common characteristics that supported that learning: Immersion in literacy is one, and the appreciation for approximations is another.

The learner "immersed in an environment where the skill is being used in purposeful ways" (Holdaway 1979, 23) learns more effectively than a child being taught isolated skills and bits of knowledge that he or she has to bring together in a social or real-life situation. Talk surrounds language learning. Children who are provided with powerful demonstrations of language have examples of how language works in situations where there is both meaning and purpose. In a kindergarten where children are immersed in texts for reading and materials for writing, they begin to think of literacy as "the way we do things around here."

Another characteristic of an authentic learning environment is one where approximation is encouraged. Successive approximation is part of learning. Even as adults we seldom learn to do things correctly the first time. Trial, error, feedback, and further trial are expected parts of literacy learning. Approximation means taking risks, having the confidence to try, and with feedback from the teacher, getting closer to being accurate. The child who scribbles "I went to the store" is approximating at writing down what they want to be read. The child who reads, "I can read to Mum" as "I like reading to my Mommy" is approximating at making meaning when reading. Children who are approximating are not just inventing or taking from thin air and applying it. They are using what they know and applying it to what is the correct convention.

Taking a risk and trying require a good attitude about learning to read and write; this attitude must be nurtured and maintained. Once this attitude is formed, then understandings become revealed as learning behaviors. Attitudes toward literacy learning are just as important to the child as the knowledge and skills the child acquires about reading and writing.

DEMONSTRATIONS

Children develop attitudes about reading and writing as they hear and watch how readers, writers, and speakers think and act. Good attitudes toward reading and writing generate confidence. Teachers can demonstrate the confidence they have as readers and writers. They can also demonstrate that risk taking and approximating are parts of learning, and that—while reading and writing is sometimes challenging—it's worth it in the end.

It is important in encouraging and maintaining children's attitudes that they participate in daily demonstrations of literacy at work. In Chapter 6, I noted a need for a space in the classroom being set aside for demonstrations. The students sit on the floor and the teacher is sitting on a low chair nearby. There is easy access to books, a chart tablet for writing, markers and white boards. This part of the room is cozy and comfortable, with enough room for all children. A cozy togetherness is important. While the teacher may be unable to replicate the intimacy of one-on-one interactions with books and print, he or she can make that experience as close to that one-on-one experience as possible. It is important to watch for the level of involvement and how active the responses are as teachers read and write in front of the students.

Demonstrations are very short at the beginning of the year, because of the length of time children can remain attentive. Teachers focus the instruction for these episodes for no longer than ten minutes.

Young children need to understand the logical connections among the literacy modes. I can model how reading and writing influence each other. I can model how reading and writing impact what we know about speaking and listening, and I can model how readers and writers can respond to what they read and write.

Teachers use rich oral and written language in their demonstrations. They show children how to look for the letters they know and the sounds they make when reading. They demonstrate the importance of making sense when reading, writing, listening, speaking, viewing, or representing. They share things learned together from the content studies and use the new vocabulary from what we have heard or read, from the books we write, and from the experiences we have shared. Expectations are demonstrated, so children understand how to use the authentic literacy environment they are now part of.

Teachers constantly make links to reading and writing.

- They talk about what the writer wants them to know as they read to the children: "I think the author asked us that question because he wants us to answer it in our heads. I wonder if we'll find the answer on the next page?" Reading is supposed to make sense to the reader. Reading causes us to ask questions of ourselves and figure out the answer.
- They think about what they want the reader to know when they demonstrate their own writing. I talk about using different words in my draft. "How could I say that so the person who reads this knows I was really scared?" I think like a writer when I read. "What could the writer have added here that might have told you more about the bear?"
- They think like readers when they write. "Wait, I left out the part about how I got there. That would be too confusing for the people who will read this."
- They know that when writers compose meaning, they ask the same questions as readers. "I wonder what this is going to be about? What do I know about this topic? What should I be thinking as I begin to read this? What's going to happen next? How do I know?"

Re-reading allows a reader and writer to ask important questions. "Does it make sense? Does it sound right? Does it look right?" Teachers provide support for these developing readers by asking themselves questions in order for their students to see how readers and writers think.

Comprehension

Comprehension is making sense of what we read. Even younger readers are already having a conversation with the writer as they read. The job of any reader is to make sense of the text and think about what he or she is reading.

Writing helps to develop comprehension. The job of any writer is to make certain the reader will make sense of what has been written. Teachers do not wait until children know sounds and letters to explore comprehension.

In summary,

- Demonstrations provide opportunities to emphasize meaning making. I understand that comprehension comes when a reader has a large oral vocabulary, so vocabulary development is part of my demonstrations.
- Demonstrations provide opportunities for the children to actively listen while I read aloud from a wide variety of texts. We have conversations before I read a book; I stop and think along the way while I read. I also talk about the words I want to use from what I read to convey meaning in my writing.

Each and every reading and writing demonstration attempts to interrelate all of the language modes.

Reading Demonstrations

Reading demonstrations are planned. The plan for reading demonstrations is based on the broad patterns and trends seen in the assessment data collected from the class (see Chapter 6). Teachers know that, for some children, the demonstrations will help consolidate skills they already have. For other children, the demonstration is a form of anticipating what they will learn next. For a few, demonstrations are the exposure to something they will take on later. Most importantly, the demonstration encourages the attitude of what it means to be a reader.

For example, from my monthly planning, I selected one particular outcome: to ask questions of myself as I read to ensure that meaning is paramount. I know that in order to achieve this outcome, my students need to use the book illustrations as a source of information for questions. My objective today is to use illustrations to ask myself questions.

Choice of books is very important. I want children to be engaged in this demonstration, to become totally involved. Engagement is a condition for learning, and for students to engage—whether it is a story or informational text—requires appealing illustrations that will raise the kinds of questions that are important to these children. I want children to listen, to think, and to respond.

My own enthusiasm about the book I select is equally important. While enjoyment is not my only teaching objective, I want these learners to believe that the umbrella for all reading is enjoyment. My own enthusiasm is a key to the development of a positive attitude toward reading.

What I know about my students and what I know about books inform my decision to select *The Little Mouse, the Red Ripe Strawberry, and the Big Hungry Bear* by Don and Audrey Wood (1984). This book has the kinds of illustrations that enable me to ask questions of myself as I read, which supports the outcome stated in my monthly plan.

This book supports my objective because:

- Both the text and illustrations cause the reader to wonder
- The illustrations are bright, clear, and easy for the children to see
- The author and illustrator have left a lot to the imagination of the reader
- I have used this book with kindergarten students before and know how appealing it is.

The book will also provide these supports and extensions:

- The language used introduces new vocabulary to the children (such as *disguised* and *guarded*).
- The innuendo in the book (an unidentified narrator who must be inferred) can extend the thinking of some children.
- The interaction between the character and the unidentified narrator creates a conceptual challenge for some children but may be recognized by others.

I can demonstrate the thinking that goes on inside a reader's head by asking aloud the kinds of questions that the illustrations suggest:

- "I wonder what's going to happen next?" develops a sense of anticipation.
- "That's an interesting word, what would that mean?" focuses on the development of vocabulary.
- "Look at this picture! That reminds me of what I saw before. I know what's going to happen now!" encourages students to use pictures as a source of information.
- "See, I knew that would happen!" confirms what the reader anticipated.
- "Hmmm... this reminds me of a time when my brother scared me..." uses prior knowledge and relates experiences to what is in the text.

Planning is how I will "think aloud" about the way a reader uses illustrations to ask questions. Here's an example of a demonstration:

I show the children the cover of the book and begin to talk.

"Look at the front of the book. What do you see on the cover?"

Many children respond... *"A mouse..."*

I continue, "He has his finger up to his mouth like this... I wonder why?"

I pause and some children talk a bit, *"It looks like he's saying, 'Sh.' "*

I continue, "I'm wondering what the title of the book might be."

I listen to children's responses, then read the title, *"The Little Mouse, the Red Ripe Strawberry, and the Hungry Bear."*

I put a puzzled look on my face, "But wait, who's missing from the cover? I don't see a bear here. I wonder what part a bear will play in the story."

I turn to the title page.

Because I am aware of the backgrounds and experiences of my students, I think about how they can be extended. I look for opportunities to make transitions between natural language and book language and how vocabulary can be developed as follows:

I continue to read about the little mouse, the hungry bear and the red strawberry, and I turn to an illustration where the mouse has the strawberry under lock and key.

I read the text, "...No matter where it is hidden, or who is guarding it."

I comment about the picture, "Look at that strawberry, it's locked up and the mouse has the key."

I use the picture to pose a question. "He must be guarding it, don't you think?"

I turn the page and continue to read, "...Or how it is disguised."

I continue to talk aloud about my thinking and how I am using the picture to connect to what I have read in the text,

"Hmmm... disguised... I wonder what that means. Let me see... the mouse has glasses and a nose on. Hey! So does the strawberry! That must be what a disguise is. It's like a mask. It tries to hide who you are. Like on Halloween."

I use the new word as I think aloud, "I don't think that disguise is working very well. I still know it's a mouse and a strawberry."

I continue to demonstrate this way—involving the children in the interaction between myself and the text.

What is important in selecting books is the way the text provides opportunities for anticipation, books that beg to be read and reread because they compel children to participate naturally. I look for books that have high-quality illustrations, books that not only give children pleasure, but are also fun for me. I find books that will engender responses through writing, art, drama, conversation, and thinking.

Reading demonstrations require an ability to throw yourself into the act of reading through action and expression, to show personal involvement with the book. That marks a teacher who doesn't just talk about children enjoying reading, but demonstrates it.

As I read, I watch children respond. Do I see behaviors that suggest a positive change in attitude? Are they eager to listen to stories and begin to chime in with the rhyme or rhythm of language? Do they automatically participate in stories and poetry? Do they begin to anticipate the emotions a book might evoke? Have they begun to develop relationships with the author of the book, knowing when to anticipate and confirm? Are they eager to return to the book after it has been read?

Demonstrations of reading help children see themselves as readers. Demonstrations of writing help children see themselves as writers.

Writing Demonstrations

Writing in front of students is also something to be done each day. Short, snappy sessions keep the children engaged. Teachers write on a large chart tablet seen by the children as the teacher's own personal draft writing book. The tablet is low enough to allow children to sit next to it on the floor or on a small chair. The writing is at the child's level.

The writing reflects what teachers expect from the children at this stage of development in the writing process. Teachers begin with a sketch, so the paper is organized by drawing a line below where the planning sketch will be. Writing is done with a black marker so it is easy to see and replicates the pencil that the child will use. We use resources that we expect the child to use, including an enlarged version of the alphabet card (see Chapters 5 and 10).

The demonstration is an opportunity for children to listen, think, and observe. The writing is mine. The teacher has the marker, and talks aloud when writing, and pauses when asking questions to encourage oral responses from the children. While we don't necessarily acknowledge each response, the children begin to see how writers can collaborate in their thinking about writing.

The demonstration is not so much *how* to write, in the sense of the knowledge and skills required for writing—though these are obviously important—but more about *what being a writer means* and *how the writing process works*. Demonstrations include—but also go beyond—the teaching of sounds and letters. Demonstrations are about having good ideas, getting them down on paper, and sharing them with others. For the teacher, this requires the same kind of enthusiasm for the process that demonstrating reading to children takes.

Similar to the reading demonstration, the objectives for the writing demonstration come from assessing the class as a whole. For example, from my monthly plan my outcome for demonstrations is to ask questions of myself as I write to ensure that meaning is paramount. Specifically, my objective for today is to ask questions of myself when planning my writing. In addition, I will be asking questions of myself as I record sounds and words as I write.

What I know about these five and six year olds guides my selection of topics for writing. Because I am aware of their self-centered world, I write mostly about myself. I write about my family, my pets, and my surroundings. I write about things that happen to me right now. I write of my own children's experiences when they were the age of these students.

My demonstration, shown in Figure 7.1, begins with how writers select topics as follows:

Figure 7.1: A Writing
Demonstration

"First I'll write the date, so I know when I wrote this piece."

I talk about my topic selection and ask myself questions as I determine my topic.

"Hmmm. What am I going to write about today? I have a couple of things I have been thinking about. I had an experience at the mall last night. I could write about that."

I hear a few children comment, *"What happened at the mall, did your car break down again?"*

I continue talking about my topic, "And then there's my dog…"

My students are used to hearing stories about my dog, so there is lots of talk about this topic. *"Foxy!!! What did Foxy do this time?"*

My topic is selected, "Yes, that's what I need to write about. This time I was lucky with Foxy. What happened was kind of funny, too."

Demonstrating writing is about:

- The thinking that goes on in a writer's head. "Something happened yesterday that I need to write about."
- Describing the thinking going on when a writer selects a topic. "Let me think about what needs to be in my sketch, so that I don't forget about the three things that happened."
- Showing how the writer organizes his or her thoughts.

I might continue my demonstration as follows:

I am organizing my thoughts. "What do I need to include in my plan?"

I provide enough information to cause them to want more. "My backyard needs to be there." I sketch as I talk.

I continue, "There's a fence around the yard. That's really important."

I can hear the children asking questions. *"Did Foxy chew stuff? I bet she chewed the bushes."* I hear their questions but do not respond. I am pleased by their natural anticipation.

I continue to sketch and talk. "Oops! Do I have Foxy in there? I almost forgot!"

The children's comments continue and are based on stories they have heard before. *"She sure gets in trouble a lot, doesn't she?"*

I put the finishing touches on my sketch. "And I need to be in there too. Now it's right."

I want my students to know that we write for a purpose and audience. "My children, Chad and Heidi, don't live at home anymore. I think they will want to read this piece. They always want to know what their dog Foxy is doing."

While the amount of text in my writing is relatively short, I am strategic in planning what I say. I am aware of the need for demonstrations in natural language. I want my writing to extend the language of these children, so I do not simplify the language or the content.

While the development of good attitudes to becoming readers and writers underlies my demonstration, skill development is important. For example, I demonstrate directionality when I see children ready for that skill in their own writing. I demonstrate how we hear and record sounds in words while I am thinking about my story.

"Let me think. What will be a good way to start my writing? I think I'll say... *I was looking out the kitchen window...* Yes, that will make the reader wonder what I'm seeing."

I demonstrate how writers write—going from sound to letter when they think about writing a word.

"*I was* (I write these two words quickly) *looking... looking*—what do I hear at the beginning of that word?"

I use an enlarged alphabet card to demonstrate connecting the sound I hear to the letter I need. "*Looking* starts like *leaf.* What letter is that?"

I point to a picture of a leaf on the alphabet card and say, "I remember, it's *l.*"

The needs of my learners determine the focus of what I say when I think aloud:

- "Let me think...*hair* starts like *hand.* What letter is that?" demonstrates a writer's need to go from sound to letter.
- "Let me read that again and see if it makes sense." confirms the need for writing to be meaningful to the reader.
- "Let me read this again to see how my illustration should look on this page." encourages writers to match the illustration and the text during the demonstration of illustrating the published text.

Writing demonstrations provide me with assessment samples about attitudes children have as developing writers. Listening to their responses as I write shows me those students who are developing the understanding of how thoughts can be written and how conventions of writing are developed. For example:

I re-read what I have written, "So what do I have so far?" I read aloud. *"I was looking out ... the...the..."* I pause. "I know that word. Let me think—how is it spelled?"

A few children chime in, *"t-h-e."*

I write *the* and continue writing... *"kitchen window when I saw ... saw..."*

Many children say, "S*! It's an* S*!"*

I write *saw* and continue, *"...Foxy trying to get out of a hole in the... fence!!!!!"*

Immediately the children begin chattering. I hear them say, *"I knew that was going to happen..." "I told you she was naughty"... "She tries to get out a lot, doesn't she?"*

I respond, "Ah—you figured it out."

Demonstrations of reading and writing bring a community of learners together. Children begin to know each other and to know me by the stories I read that we love. Together we read stories that have wonderful illustrations, that make us laugh, that connect to our own experiences, that tell us things, and that have us ask questions. The children know me also through my writing demonstrations in which I have shared family stories, stories of the past, and things I wonder about. Demonstrations are often like conversations among a group of friends.

The Power of Demonstration on Children's Learning

In my students' reading and writing I look to see evidence of growth, how their attitudes about reading, writing, and learning are becoming developed and maintained. I watch, listen, and record what I see and hear as evidence of what they now know.

Set out in Figure 7.2 is a selection of my observations in various classroom spaces and the monitoring notes I recorded about my students attitudes as their literacy learning develops.

My goal is to develop, build, and maintain these kindergartners' confidence as readers, writers, listeners, speakers, and viewers. An effective tool for achieving that goal is my daily demonstration as a reader and writer at work. Once confidence is developed, the potential for growth is limitless. Demonstrations occur because the information I have collected about the children guides my instruction.

"Julio, what's this band aid doing on your elbow?"
"I fell down on my steps last night."
"I bet that hurt."
"It did, but I didn't even cry. I just told my dad. I'm going to write about that today."
"I liked the way you said—'I didn't even cry.' That sounds like you're really growing up. You might want to put that in your story."
"I am growing up. My dad said so."

I note: "Julio confidently chooses topics."

Kyle rushes to me, saying, *"You are not going to believe this! My last name is the same as my dad's—every single letter!"*

I note: "Kyle understands print is constant and provides a message."

I listen to conversations in the classroom library ... Two children are reading a book that I read to them a few days ago. *"This is the funny part... look here—where he says 'Lotta water!!,"* Both children erupt with laughter.

I write: "Sophie and Anna return to books and express opinions."

Keisha is reading *Jesse Bear, What Will You Wear* ..., a book that I have read to the class repeatedly since the first day of school. She is sitting on a small chair, the book held just as I hold it when reading aloud to the students— with the pictures facing front. *"Jesse Bear, Jesse Bear—What are you wearing today? You best get dressed now, it's time for you to leave for school."*

I note: "Keisha can use the pictures to tell the story."

Several children are working with the flannel board characters from *Mrs. Wishy Washy*, a book they have read and re-read in the classroom. I hear *"Wishy, washy, wishy, washy"* repeatedly.

I note: "Quenton and Jazz are using rhyme and rhythm from books."

Jaren is writing about his dog trying to bury a bone in the house. He is subvocalizing as he writes. *"Jack—/j/."* He writes J. *"Jack—/a/. What makes /a/?"* He looks at the alphabet card and says, *"Oh, yeah! Apple."* He writes a. Then he quickly writes c. He takes a look at it and says, *"Hey! I know how to write Jack!"*

Children are on the playground. They are huddled together, looking at a bee on the bushes. I overhear Colin say, *"A big body and tiny wings... How does the bumblebee fly?,"* a line from a book we've read in class.

I note: "Colin is using book language in oral language and applying what has been read to a real-life situation."

I note: "Jaren is confident in recording the sounds he hears and checking with what he knows."

Figure 7.2: Collected Data Informing Demonstrations

8   developing
the knowledge and skills
of the emergent learner

This chapter explores the teacher's role in developing the knowledge and skills of students moving through the emergent stage of the literacy continuum and describes the kinds of support provided.

STRUCTURES TO SUPPORT AND SCAFFOLD LEARNING

Literacy learning begins at birth. As we have seen, when children enter kindergarten they are at varying points along the literacy continuum. Most will be at what we define as the emergent stage. At this stage of their literacy development, the members of the class have similar learning needs, yet require different levels of support. By adjusting the support, teachers provide a scaffold for the learner but "scaffolding does not mean simplifying the task; it holds the task difficulty constant while simplifying the child's role by means of graduated assistance from the adult" (Tharp and Gallimore 1993, 33).

As I observe children who are learning to write in lowercase letters, I reflect on differing levels of support they need. For one child, simply observing my use of lowercase letters in a writing demonstration is sufficient. Another child begins to take it on when I talk through the use of lowercase letters as I write my demonstration piece. Another uses lowercase letters when I remark in front of the group how many students I have seen using them. The shift is made by another child after we count how many uppercase and lowercase letters are on the page of one of their favorite books. Yet another starts writing in lowercase letters once I show her how to start using them. There is one child who begins to use them when she hears me congratulating another child. There's no one way for every child!

All of this information helps plan instructional time. Whole group demonstrations are an efficient and effective way to show students how readers read and how writers write, but the diverse needs of the learners cannot be supported through whole group instruction alone. Increasing the knowledge and skills of students means providing instruction in small groups and to individual children. Grouping allows the teacher to watch and listen. Clay comments that "teaching...can be likened to a conversation in which you listen to the speaker carefully before you reply" (1985, 6). Because the teacher watches and listens, teaching becomes a conversation between the teacher and the learner. By listening carefully, the teacher is supporting individual learning.

Learning occurs best when a special relationship develops between the students and the teacher. Teachers observe children's interactions with them, with the learning experience, and with other students. They listen to what each child says. The children begin to understand the teacher's role in their learning. The information seen and heard helps determine the appropriate response to scaffold their learning. As the teacher responds, he or she watches and listens again to judge the effectiveness of the instruction. Through those interactions, the instruction begins to ebb and flow, allowing the teacher to adjust the support. Support is adjusted for the group and for individuals. The path for learning is smoothed.

MANAGING LEARNING AT THE EMERGENT STAGE OF LITERACY

Figure 8.1 is a teaching plan for a day in the third month of school. I have completed the writing and reading demonstration and the children are now working on various literacy activities throughout the classroom. Some are writing. Some are in the classroom library. Two are engaged in an alphabet game. Three are with a story at the listening post. A few are illustrating books that I published with them yesterday. Another small group is using a magnifying glass to look at some insects that arrived in a jar this morning. Two children are lying on the floor turning the pages of an enlarged text and a group is retelling a familiar story with flannel board figures. It is time for me to get busy.

I plan my time in twenty-minute blocks, and then I pull the whole group of children together for a story, some songs and poetry, or a bit of outside play. We return to what we were doing for another twenty-minute block. As the children's literacy skills increase, they are able to sustain independent work over longer periods of time.

Literacy Planning for Date: __October 7__   # DAILY PLAN

WRITING DEMONSTRATION	READING DEMONSTRATION	SONGS/POETRY
Obj: To listen, identify, record initial sounds. Topic: Birthday Party	Obj: To use pictures to anticipate. Text: Bear Wants More (Karma Wilson)	If You're Happy and You Know It Head, Shoulders, Knees, Toes Down By the Station

Small Group Instruction

READING	READING	WRITING	ALPHABET
Obj: Word-by-word matching Group: Alberto, Keisha, Jazz, Julio, Marcy Resource: My Little Brother Ben	Obj: Directionality (L to R) Group: Celia, Jaren, Kyle, Maria Resource: The Fox	Obj: Adding onto writing Group: Nina, José Resource: Draft Book	Obj: To match pictures to letters Group: Janisha, Caleb, Jasmine, Quenton, Beau Resource: Alphabet Card Memory Game

Publishing

NAME TEACHING POINT	Spelling	Oral Reading
*Celia → add to plan *Jaren → L to R *Maria → talk about plan *Kyle → plan matches writing *Janisha → plan matches writing *Caleb → plan matches writing *Jasmine → oral language/L to R *Quenton → L to R Paul → word "I" Julio → endings of words Marcy → oral rehearsal Dani → initial sounds * Daily	Colin Julio	Dani Beau

	Monitoring Learning
	Focus: Story structure - classroom library puppets Who? Anna, Caleb, Maria, Jaren, Paul

NOTES

Figure 8.1: Planning for a Day in the Third Month of School

THE CHILD AS THE GUIDE

Managing the learning of more than twenty children each day means that I look for teaching approaches that allow me many points of entry for instruction. Sylvia Ashton-Warner was a teacher who worked with young children coming to school with limited language experiences. She used the students' prior experiences to develop them as readers and writers. She writes, "Back to these first words, to these first books; they must be made of the stuff of the child itself... I reach a hand into the mind of the child, bring out a handful of the stuff I find there, and use it as our first working material" (Ashton-Warner 1963, 34).

Children always come to school with "stuff" they are anxious to talk about. Talking comes before, and accompanies, reading and writing. I use the strength in oral language as the foundation for the support I can provide. It is important to respect children's natural language and use it, for example, as they get their ideas down in a sketch for their daily draft book writing. These sketches allow the child to organize what they will eventually write. Setting out their story correctly makes the student story "public" so that others can read it. Publishing student writing and using the publishing episode to extend and further develop language structures is another opportunity to scaffold literacy learning. The publication becomes a small book illustrated by the student and the initial independent reading material for the child.

The following sections illustrate my work with an emergent group of children where I use their daily writing to expand their experiences of speaking, reading, and writing through the publication of their stories.

Daily writing is housed in a draft writing book. The draft writing book keeps student writing in one place. It provides evidence of student growth over time, and it is a place for me to record the growth I observe in the student's knowledge and skills. The draft writing book is as much my management tool as it is the place where students write.

STRUCTURES FOR PUBLISHING WRITING

Blank Books

For emergent readers and writers, daily writing results in a published book. I carry blank books with me as I move about the room (see Figure 8.2). A blank book has several pages stapled together. These books are different sizes and shapes and open like a "real" book allowing the child to go from front to back as they read. The paper is of good quality to avoid printing or illustrations that bleed through the page and cause confusion. My handwriting is large and clear. I want these books to provide a model for the child.

Figure 8.2. Blank Book Example

Students who are emerging as writers are also emerging as readers. High-quality texts formatted for emergent readers provide a model for the way I publish. For the child who is developing the concept that print goes from left to right, it is important to publish with one line of text on each page. For the child who understands this concept and is now learning the return sweep, left to right, it is helpful to publish two lines of text on each page. For children who are learning word-by-word matching, the print needs to be high enough on the page for the child to point underneath the words. The print is written in appropriate chunks so that the child can reinterpret the meaning through illustrations. Page and line breaks are carefully planned to respect the natural language of the child.

Using the Alphabet Card

Each child has an alphabet card (see Figure 8.3). The alphabet card has features that support the development of sound-to-letter relationships (Clay 1991).

For example, I know that going from the known to the unknown is an easier process for any learner. Children typically are able to say a word before they can write it. Therefore, going from the sounds the child can say to writing down the

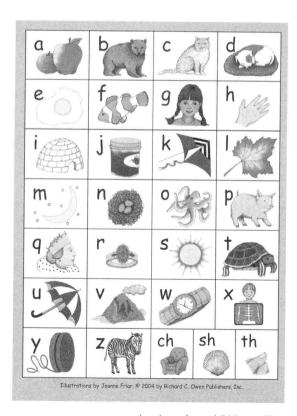

Illustrations by Joanne Friar. © 2004 by Richard C. Owen Publishers, Inc.

Figure 8.3: Alphabet Card

letter or clusters of letters that make the sound is easier than going from an isolated letter and trying to remember its sound.

The alphabet card links a familiar picture to the sound and the letter. The link between the picture and the letter needs to be clear for the child, so it can be used almost immediately. The pictures are of objects that children can identify. I hear children saying, "*Mom* starts like *moon*—here it is!"

The letters on the child-sized card are lowercase only. Children usually come to school writing in capital letters. Writers use capital letters for specific purposes, so I want these students to make the shift to writing in lowercase as quickly as possible.

In addition to single letters, the alphabet card I use also shows three diagraphs (*ch, th, sh*). These combined letters have a unique sound that cannot be segmented when the child is listening for sounds in words. The alphabet card provides support for the child with pictures for common diagraphs *ch—chair, sh—shell, th—thumb*.

Familiarity with the alphabet card at the beginning of the year is encouraged by playing alphabet games with the whole class, working with the card in small groups, and using the enlarged card in my own writing demonstrations. This card should quickly become a valuable resource for both teacher and child.

Planning Ideas for Writing

I understand that "the writer cannot build a good, strong, sturdy piece of writing unless he has gathered an abundance of fine raw material" (Murray 1968). Children plan their writing by drawing a pencil sketch. A sketch depicts graphically the thoughts and ideas the child plans to include in the piece of writing. It is brainstorming for the emergent writer, and it enables them to remember what they have decided to write about. I can use the sketch as one entry point of instruction to build on their developing oral language.

I know which children need my support while they are choosing topics and sketching ideas. My time with these children is short and to the point, but I am showing genuine interest in what they are writing about and what they intend to say. Daily writing provides a window into a child's life. The more they write, the more I know about them and the more meaningful my interactions can be. The following examples show how oral language can be developed from talking about what the children are going to write about.

Jasmine

Jasmine is a new learner of English whose receptive language is quite good and whose expressive language is developing. I look at the sketch in her draft book

Figure 8.4: Jasmine's Sketch

and see the same picture she has drawn for a number of days; her Mama. I ask her what she is writing about and she tells me, "Mama."

I want her to understand that a story is about more than just the character; it's the character's actions as well. I know that she needs more language to be able to describe the actions of the character. I see her sketch as the vehicle to link the action to the words she needs. I ask her, "What is your Mama doing?"

Jasmine replies, "Tamales."

We talk about what her Mama is doing and determine she is cooking tamales. I suggest she add details to her plan that will show her Mama cooking: the pan, the tamales, the stove. Jasmine adds those details and I name the items she is adding as she draws.

When she finishes I say, "Those pictures will help you remember what your Mama is cooking in your story. What will your story say?"

Jasmine replies, "Mama—tamales."

I model for Jasmine the language structure she needs to tell a story that will not only make sense but sound right, "So your story will say, 'My Mama cooks tamales!' That will make everyone hungry. Tell me what your story will say?"

Jasmine says, "My Mama cooks tamales."

"That sounds right!" I reply, " Write that down and I'll be back to see how you're doing."

I check back in a few minutes to monitor her progress and to provide assistance as needed.

The support I am providing for her with vocabulary and language structure will lessen as she gains more control of English.

Caleb

Young children take comfort in what they know, and they repeat similar episodes through writing. Caleb writes about his dog each day. I want him to extend his thinking by extending his plan for writing.

I ask him a few questions to find the "nugget," his real story. "Where is your dog in the story, Caleb?" I ask.

Caleb responds and points to the grass and trees in his sketch, "In my backyard."

"I'm wondering what he's doing in your backyard?" I continue. Unlike Jasmine, Caleb has the oral English to describe the action in his story and needs to be encouraged to represent what he can say in his sketch.

He replies, "Hiding in the doghouse 'cause the rain is coming down."

I've found the "nugget" in Caleb's story and uncovered some interesting language; 'hiding in the doghouse' brings voice to this piece of writing. I encourage him to add some details to his plan; the doghouse and the rain. Figure 8.5 shows the changes in Caleb's sketch as a result of this instruction.

All children write in their draft book daily, and each child is viewed as a writer regardless of their current stage along the literacy continuum. I accept any form the writing takes and proceed from there. Emergent writers scribble, make letter-like forms, and write random strings of letters. As they move through the emergent stage, more of the letters they write will have a corresponding sound, and I expect to see them use words they know how to write and read.

While the students are drafting, I move about the room observing and interacting with children to determine if they are using what they have been taught. Their different stages on the literacy continuum mean I monitor different things with individual children. I may be monitoring directionality with Jaren, initial sounds with Carlos, the word *I* with Celia, and spaces between words with Julio. I re-teach, remind, or instruct as needed. At the same time, I am checking back to see they are following through on the responsibility to use their new learning.

Figure 8.5: Caleb's Changing Plan as the Result of Instruction

Paul

Paul has entered school as an emergent writer. He produces lines of scribble and some random strings of letters as he writes (see Figure 8.6). Paul writes from left to right with a return sweep on each new line. He is using some letter-like forms (including a *P*, which is the initial letter of his first name). When I ask him to read his writing, he responds this way:

"I have a sister who is a cheerleader, and I go to my sister's school on Friday night and watch her cheer at the football game at Wilson High School, and she throws her pom-poms in the air, and the stuff flies all over the place, and she goes to practice a lot, and I go with my Mom and Dad to the game, and I get a Coke at halftime."

Paul's sketch matches his writing. Paul understands how to tell a story and his oral language is more developed than his written language right now. For Paul to read his published book, it will need to be short and to the point yet carry the sense of the story. I say to Paul, "Oh, so your story is, 'I have a sister who is a cheerleader.' Let's publish that."

Figure 8.6: Paul's Plan
and Writing

I publish Paul's book so that he will be able to read and reread this story. I know this little book will be one of many that aid in the development of left to right and return sweep, one-to-one matching, sound/symbol relationships and words he needs to know. I select a teaching point for Paul for this publishing episode: to learn to read and write the word *I*.

I show Paul the text of his last three stories ("I have a cat named Murray," "I like my new lunchbox," " I went to my Grammie's house"). We talk about how often he uses the word *I* in his writing, and I tell him that it's a word he needs to know.

I teach Paul the letter formation while I am instructing, "Straight down, across at the top, across at the bottom," I say. He practices by writing *I* on the table with his finger, on the back of my hand, and on a page in his draft book.

At this point, I pull out a blank book and marker, and we publish his story. We begin by reading it together from his draft book. "I have a sister who is a cheerleader." We talk about the first word, *I*, the word he has just learned. I write the word *I* after our conversation, then quickly write down the rest of the story.

This booklet forms part of the first reading material available to Paul for independent reading. Children bring to the reading of their books a wealth of prior knowledge. The story was their experience. They have written about it. We talk about the content of the illustration and the materials they need. Now Paul has the opportunity to read and reread these familiar texts.

I will look for Paul's knowledge of what has been taught as he rereads his published book and the trade books I select for instructional group work. Is he using the word *I* in his writing on a consistent basis? Is he able to identify the word *I* in his reading and use it as he approximates at word-by-word matching?

Dani

Dani has shifted from only using scribbles in her writing to using the word *I*. She uses some letters in her name as she writes and also uses random strings of letters and letter-like forms.

I ask Dani to tell me about her sketch, shown in Figure 8.7. She says, "This is me and my mom and my dog. We had to take him to the doctor because he hurt his leg. He didn't want to go." I ask Dani to read what she has written. She points and reads, "I took my dog to the doctor with my mom. He didn't want to go."

Figure 8.7: Dani's Sketch
and Writing

Dani's writing and what she reads are my assessment sample. I make a quick decision about what I see her doing, what she is attempting to do, and what she needs to do next, all in order to determine my teaching point for publication. Dani is using the word *I* appropriately. She writes in random strings of letters but some are the letters in her first and last name.

She writes about herself and her family frequently. She uses the words *me* and *my* and *mom* in her writing. She is ready to learn initial sounds. I can quickly teach her the sound and symbol for the letter *m* and expect that she will use this sound in her writing when she writes on these familiar topics.

I say to Dani, "I knew this story started with the word *I* because you wrote it right here in your draft book."

I expect Dani to be looking at what I'm doing on the page as I publish. "Watch Dani, you wrote, 'I took' " ... I quickly write those two words because my focus will be on the sound and letter *m*. "The next word you wrote was *my*. You use that word a lot in your writing. You write about 'my sister, my new baby, and my uncle fixing the car.' " I show her these stories in her draft book. I continue, "Listen to me say that word *my*." I say the word slowly. "You say the word, Dani," I continue.

Dani says the word. Next I say, "Now listen carefully. What do you hear at the beginning of the word?" I pull out Dani's alphabet card. "Let's find the picture on your alphabet card that begins with the same sound as *my*," I say. Dani hesitates.

I point to the letter *m* on the alphabet card and say, "*My* starts like *moon*. What letter is that?" Dani responds with the letter name and I write *m* in her published book. Her response to my question, "What letter is that?" is another assessment sample. If Dani knows the name of the letter, I focus on the sound and letter formation. If Dani does not know the letter, I teach the letter name as well.

I reinforce this instruction as I write the words *my* and *mom*. This instruction is intentional and focused. What makes it intentional is my knowledge of what Dani knows and what she needs to know. I make a note that she can identify this initial sound through listening and can name the letter that starts the word. I record what has been taught.

Dani's book becomes an opportunity for reading instruction as well. I ask her to read her book to me and to remember to point to the words as she reads. Her directionality and return sweep are consolidated. Her one-to-one matching is developing.

I quickly take her back to the previous instruction and say, "Good reading, Dani, show me that letter you learned today." Dani points to the letter *m* in *my*. "Read your story again and make sure your finger is on the *m* when you say that word *my*," I say.

I expect Dani to be successful with this because of the placement of the word *my* on the page. She knows the story. She knows where to start, knows the word *I* and the *m* comes soon after with multiple opportunities for practice. I expect that letter (and soon *the*) to become accurately written anchors for her work toward word-by-word matching.

We finish our publication with a brief conversation about illustrations. Once again, I use what I know about quality books for children at the emergent stage on the continuum; the importance of the picture matching the text, and enhancing the meaning of the story.

As Dani reads each page, "I took my dog to the doctor with my mom." I ask her how she will illustrate them, "What will be a good picture for this page?"

Dani is accustomed to making some decisions about her illustrations. She knows the illustration should match the words. She decides if she will use colored pencils, crayons, or markers for the pictures. When she finishes her illustrations, she puts her book in a basket by my chair and I read it to the class just like I read a book by any author.

THE POWER OF PUBLICATION

At the beginning of the year, I want to publish every child's writing while the child is alongside. The information I learn from my interaction with the child provides valuable assessment data. From the analysis of that data, I come to understand where each child is on the literacy continuum. It's only through knowing each child that I can proceed rapidly and with efficiency to ensure that new learning occurs every day.

In the twenty minutes of classroom time working with these students, I was able to provide the following support for:

- Jasmine in her oral language development by modeling the sentence structure "My mama cooks tamales."
- Caleb to add detail to his plan for writing.
- Paul in narrowing his topic and teaching the word *I*.
- Dani in learning the sound to symbol and letter formation of the letter *m*.

> ## PUBLISHING WORK INSTEAD OF WRITING IN THE STUDENT DRAFT BOOK
>
> I am sometimes asked why I choose to publish students' writing as a booklet rather than write in the draft writing book. My reasons can be summarized as follows:
>
> - I can publish an individual little book in the time it would take me to write the same text in the draft book.
>
> - I want the published books to become the independent reading material for the child.
>
> - I publish to enable children to easily read what they have written. I use clear text, large spaces between words, room under the text for word-by-word matching, one or two lines of text based on the reader's stage of development. This work provides the correct model.
>
> - I want to avoid the message that might occur when I write under their writing, "Tell me your story and I'll write it for you" because of the dependence it can create.
>
> I do use the pages in the student draft book to teach letter formation, essential words, where to begin, and spacing between words because of the convenience and because it can become a resource for the writer.

In addition to that, I was able to touch base with Jaren to monitor left to right directionality in his reading. I was able to see if Carlos was using the letter *t*, which was introduced yesterday. At the same time I checked Celia's use of the word *I* and Julio's consistent use of spaces between words.

WORKING WITH SMALL GROUPS

In Chapter 5, I discussed the importance of small groups and why they are an organizational tool for managing learning. Planning for small groups requires preparation.

Many kindergarten children come to school quite comfortable with having a book on their laps. They have had the benefit of bedtime story experiences. These opportunities for reading provided the child with access to the print, the illustrations, and the wide-ranging discussions that evolved during the bedtime story experience. Those interactions were significant in the growth and development of what they understood about literacy when they arrived at school. Most of my children feel like readers.

My challenge has been to replicate that bedtime experience in the classroom. Not only do I need to make up for lost time with children who have had minimal experiences with rich literacy activities, but I also need to maintain the confidence of those who have come to school feeling like readers and writers. How can I make those experiences even more powerful and even more focused than the bedtime story? How can I make certain that small group reading is meaningful and enjoyable and kindles the enthusiasm and confidence these children have as readers?

Selecting the Objective—What Do I Want Them to Learn?

I ask myself, "What do I know about these learners? What evidence do I have of that knowledge? What learning do I expect to occur from this teaching experience? Will I be meeting the needs of my students? Where is the entry point for the group? Where are the entry points for the individual child?" The answer to these questions allows me to select an objective for the group based on my observation. My objective with this particular group of children is to use pictures to anticipate.

Selecting the Resource or Learning Experience— What Tools Will Assist in the Learning?

Now I must think about the resource or learning experience. I carefully select the text based on the needs of the group of children I have brought together. I determine the features of the text that will support what they know and what they need to know. While I understand the need for simplicity, I will identify books with the kind of challenges that have the best potential for helping children to become successful readers. I want these books to engender questions, invite responses, and arouse or satisfy curiosity.

I identify the supports and challenges the book offers children. I know that the supports and challenges in books will differ from child to child, depending upon what they know at that particular time. I look for books that:

- Allow the reader to be successful
- Contain a strong story line, often revealed as much through the pictures as the text
- Are supportive page by page but also throughout the text
- Have a logical beginning, middle, and end

- Portray themes familiar and sensitive to five- and six-year-old children: family, children, pets, school
- Contain pictures that allow the reader to predict the story line
- Have one or two lines of print, placed consistently at the bottom of the page
- Have larger print with wide spaces between words and a large white space at the bottom of the page to support finger, voice, print match
- Contain more supports than challenges for the reader.

I have single copies of books and I also have enlarged texts (Big Book editions of the same titles). I ask myself more questions. Will I be able to get the same level of discussion if the children each have their own book? Will the children be able to see the print, the illustration, and the conventions of print if I use a Big Book? Will they be close enough to the text to feel they are part of it?

The Size of the Group—How Many or How Few to Maximize Learning?

This leads me to the question of the size of the group. Will the group be too large for me to be able to observe student behavior? Will I be able to participate in the same kind of intimate discussion that takes place during the bedtime story? Will I have the opportunity to listen to what each child is wondering about in the text? Will I be in the position to support the problem solving that may need to occur? Will I be able to respond to the identified needs of each child? Can I reach my objective in a timely manner, so that the other children in the classroom are able to sustain their independent work?

Reading instruction occurs in small groups formed by the identified needs of the learners. The number of students in the group is directly related to the amount of support needed and the age and stage of development of the child. Three to five children are an optimal size depending upon the task at hand.

The Amount, Timing, and Nature of Support

When determining a length of time for instruction, *short* is the term to remember. I have experienced five-minute instructional episodes that have been very effective. No lesson needs to be longer than ten minutes when the objective is focused. Because I know that I will probably be meeting this group again for more work on the same objective, instruction can be short, snappy, and to the point.

I provide maximal support when I know that the children bring less experience to the learning of this new skill. Children who come to school without a well-developed literacy set need frequent, powerful literacy experiences. The aim is to accelerate their learning to a level similar to those who have had five years of school-like literacy experiences. Small group instruction is one tool that will enable me to provide opportunities for this catch-up. These interactions between the children, the text, and me are not random events, but are carefully engineered and executed instructional episodes. I am accelerating the learning of these children, so the opportunities for instruction are frequent.

While setting expectations that learning will occur, I create an environment of learning and support. I may sit on the floor with children. I may sit at a small table. I prefer a round table to a kidney shaped table or a rectangular table because I want the feeling of thinking and talking our way through the text together, rather than the conversation being directed to and from me. Regardless of my objective for instruction, I realize that reading for meaning is paramount, so I want to establish a tone where students can anticipate, wonder, think, and talk about the meaning they are creating.

Conversation is imperative. With young children, conversation is their strength; a child less experienced with books and print can still communicate with me and the rest of the group about what they know through talk. My ability to genuinely and actively listen is heavily tested in an active classroom of five year olds. I must perfect the art of looking at the speaker and genuinely hearing what they have to say.

I begin talking with the children about the expectations in the group, "We're going to read one of my favorite books today. Who can help us remember where our eyes need to be when we read." I want them to understand the expectations each time we sit together with a book.

I continue with a focus on the title, "The title of this book is *Mr. Gumpy's Outing* (Burningham 1971). I wonder what it's going to be about?" I find out about what each child knows when I listen carefully. The children respond.

"I think that guy is Mr. Gumpy," Kyle comments. I ask him what makes him say that and he replies, *"He's the biggest one, so he would be the Mister."*

I continue, "So we think Mr. Gumpy will be in the book. Do you have any other ideas?" The children are very quiet.

Initially the children require significant adult support. I use my own voice to support the reading. The child's eyes are on the print and there will be opportunities for student participation. My oral reading will be at a pace to support these readers. As I read, I watch very closely the responses of each child to the task at hand. I adjust the support accordingly. I encourage conversations about what is happening in the book and what the children think will happen next. Through talk, I link what they are reading to the background knowledge they bring to the book.

I provide some additional support, "Where might I look to get ideas about the book? Where did you look, Kyle, when you told us who might be Mr. Gumpy?"

Kyle tells us he looked at the picture, which allows me to bring out my teaching point of using the pictures to anticipate. "So the picture gives us ideas about what we might read. Hmmm… what does the picture make us think?" I ask. One child points to the boat, and our conversation continues as we begin to wonder about the boat.

"I wonder how he got the animals in that boat."

"I think there are too many animals!"

"What if they fall out and drown?"

This is exactly what I want the children to do, pose questions in anticipation of what they will read in the text.

I encourage, explain, and provide demonstrations where needed. I take every opportunity to use what the text has to offer to increase the knowledge of these children about how books work, how stories are structured, and what vocabulary can be learned. Skills are taught with a focus. Understandings are developed within these engaging reading, writing, and talking experiences.

I use instructional opportunities to invite inexperienced readers into the world of what readers do. I provide adequate support for the reading and the scaffold for these learners as I do the reading and they do the thinking. They think about how the picture supports their thinking, how the story confirms what they predicted, how the reading involves lots of thinking and lots of enjoyment.

I watch and listen for children applying what they begin to know. I want them to practice those skills in an environment that is supportive and enjoyable.

I understand that pausing or hesitating while I read invites the children to use what they have begun to know to predict at the word level. Reading part of the sentence and stopping before a selected word enables students to use their own language system to "induce the response." That means "whenever it is possible to induce the desired process, rather than give instructions on how to carry it out, this is more efficient method of teaching. Induction is more efficient than instruction" (Holdaway 1980).

I read, "The rabbit hopped."

"The children squabbled."

"The boat" ...I pause and this time the children make a number of predictions.

"Dumped," "Fell over," "I was right! I said they would fall in."

I continue to read, "tipped..."

I turn the page and the children burst into laughter and conversation.

Conducting small group instruction with young children who have limited experiences is sometimes quite a feat. I have lamented the fact that I do not have more hands, as I try to keep each child on the same page, watch for one-to-one matching, and have a meaningful conversation about the book while everyone's bottom stays on the floor. I act upon what I hear and see while I am teaching.

Much of the assessment that I do is on the run. This five- or ten-minute lesson also gives me data that will inform the next meeting of this group. My eyes and ears are open to see what the learner can do and is attempting to do, but I am rarely able to record any observations until after the group is finished. I take a couple of minutes at the end of the group and write down what I have now learned:

- Caleb, Janisha, Quenton—use pictures to predict, read along
- Jasmine—shows engagement through laughter
- Beau—uses pictures to predict, contributes to the discussion, reads along.

Do these children need more opportunities with text like the one used for instruction today? Absolutely, and over time I would expect that the amount of support provided through the conversation will shift and change.

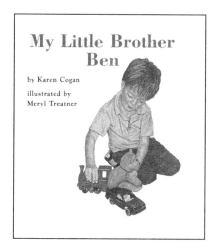

Figure 8.8: *My Little Brother Ben*

As I work alongside children in my kindergarten, I find that what they are learning about writing also helps their reading. What I see them use in their draft books—such as initial letters of words—I also hear them applying in small group reading instruction. My teaching plan now is to bring a small group together to teach word-by-word matching. I have recorded evidence about what these children can do. I know they have a good attitude about reading. They enjoy being asked to participate in a small group and are eager to know what the book will be about. This group of students knows that the print contains a message, where the print is, and that it goes from left to right. I know that when I ask, "Where do you start when you read?" these children put their finger at the beginning of the sentence.

There are four students in this small group. While the objective (word-by-word matching) is the same for each child in the group, the support I provide depends upon the knowledge the learner brings to this skill. What I know about these students impacts all decisions I make, even where they will sit in the group. We sit in a circle on the floor. I intentionally seat Celia and Jaren across from me because they will most likely need gentle reminders of where their fingers need to go, and I will be able to monitor their progress with my eyes. Kyle is sitting to my left and Maria is sitting on my right. I know that both of these learners may need more direct support with my hand guiding their finger from time to time. I expect the support I provide for Celia and Jaren will be to encourage and moni-tor. I select a book where the text placement varies on one page to offer a chal-lenge. "Where does your finger go when you read? Then which way do you go?" may be the only reminder those two children need.

While the task is the same, my support for Alan and Maria is different. I will encourage and explain, and I may need to share the task. "Where does your fin-ger go when you read? Then where will you go?" I expect this is a skill they know. If not, I'm prepared to place their fingers on the correct place and gently move them from left to right. As an additional support, I have a small chart tablet beside me to record information that helps support the meaning that the children are making as they read.

I read aloud and they read with me. We converse about the content of the book. The challenge I expect them to take on is word-by-word matching. I watch how they are doing. In some places I may slow the pace of my reading to maximize their success.

Meaning is the reason we read. I spend time setting the stage for reading. I ask the children what the cover makes them think about. I listen to their responses to determine how much scene-setting is required and how much background they bring to this text. They all talk of the experiences they have had with block building.

"I see a boy playing with blocks. We have those blocks in my daycare."

"We have blocks like that in this school, right over there!"

"Sometimes, when we build with blocks, they all crash down!"

"It sounds as if you think the blocks will have something to do with this story, and you talked about the blocks 'crashing down,' because that's something that can happen with blocks."

The conversation continues, with other children adding what they have done with blocks.

I make certain that the umbrella outcome overarching every small group meeting is meaning. What meaning do I anticipate can be made with this text? What rich oral language will it promote? I read the book first as a reader, to answer these questions. I read the book again as a teacher, to determine the entry points for instruction.

I draw attention to the boy on the cover, and the discussion shifts to problems with little brothers or sisters. Two of the children have younger siblings. One is a younger sibling. All have something to share. We talk about potential problems with the brothers and the blocks. Our work with word-by-word matching occurs throughout the book, but meaning is the overarching reason we learn any new skills.

I also use an oral reading record to check what the learner is beginning to understand. These oral reading records are scheduled as part of my daily plan and are taken every three weeks on a kindergarten child. Because I expect the students' learning to develop rapidly, this is one way to monitor their progress toward a set for literacy. At this stage of development, the oral reading record is analyzed for the behaviors that constitute a literacy set (see Chapter 6, Figure 6.6).

When young children realize they will read and write daily, they begin to talk like readers and writers and behave like readers and writers. I use the language of the processes to clarify what we are doing and why we are doing it. We talk about selecting topics for writing and making predictions in reading. We discuss what we think the author of the book wants us to know and do, and we talk about who we think will want to read the books we write. I explain and clarify as I teach so the children understand that what they are learning will make reading, writing, listening, speaking, and viewing easier for them. I have learned that these kindergarteners begin to value what I value in literacy. They attend to what I attend to.

Time has carefully been planned in my classroom, with the student needs at the forefront. I use time to build and maintain attitudes about literacy through demonstrations. I use time to increase the knowledge and skills of my kindergarten students through small group and individual instruction. And I use time to build the Essential Skills (Ministry of Education 1993)—the skills for life—through independent work.

CONSOLIDATING THE LEARNING THROUGH APPLICATION AND PRACTICE

Instruction alone does not solidify or consolidate learning. Children need time to use what they have been taught. Practice influences competence. These young learners have practiced talking, climbing, door opening, bike riding, block building, booting up the computer, or using the remote control before they have come to school. Their proficiency is a result of the practice they have had. I provide opportunities for these children to use what they are learning.

Chapter 5 focused on the classroom as a center for learning. The classroom has been organized to manage student learning. Time is set aside for children to read, write, talk, and respond to the literacy teaching that has occurred. Materials have been organized to be easily accessible to the child. Expectations have been set. The environment reflects how I have planned for children to use what has been taught. The classroom is the workplace where children learn not only academic skills but also develop the Essential Skills, the skills for life (Ministry of Education 1993, 17). The skills I closely monitor during independent time are:

- Communication Skills
- Information Skills
- Problem-solving Skills
- Self-management Skills
- Social and Cooperative Skills
- Work and Study Skills.

These skills are interconnected in the kindergarten classroom. Marie Clay points out that "learning in one area enriches the potential for learning in other areas. There must be room for a child to make discoveries, must be opportunities for conflicts to surface and be resolved in the making or the discussion or the presentation to others" (1998, 190). Children learn more about talking by having experiences in reading and writing. They learn more about reading by dramatizing a story, drawing a picture, or making something out of clay. I provide the opportunities to foster independence in the way the child attends to the task. I provide some support along the way for the child to make the connections.

I gather the information through this big picture of learning the essential skills. I monitor how the child uses what has been taught under the umbrella of the six areas described previously. I look for evidence that they use these new skills automatically and with some fluency. I search for confirmation that the child is applying the new learning to different situations. I use these opportunities to gather assessments. I determine where more support is needed, and I monitor and extend the learning of the child.

As the school year continues, I look beyond these obvious literacy skills to how the children are operating in the classroom. I look for their ability to *gather information*. What do I expect to see from these kindergarteners at the emergent stage? The way children use pictures as they explore books, use the listening post, or look at materials in the discovery area all will show me what they know about gathering information. I listen to children's conversations and how they are able to listen to their peers. My students' independent writing indicates the automatic use of the alphabet card to gather information about a letter they need. I wonder how they access other resources in the room for reading and writing.

I'm interested in the child's ability to *problem solve* at this stage of development. I'm not only observing how they access materials they need, find places to sit, and which book to choose, but I'm also watching how they determine what topic to choose for writing, or what to do when they come to something they don't know. I'm aware of the number of problems that need to be solved by these five year olds: What letter makes that sound? What sound does that letter make? How do I write that letter? What is that letter? What do I need to do next? I look for a shift in the independence of these children to solve their own problems.

I expect to see more independence in how the children *manage themselves*. I determine the personal investment children have in their student plan. I watch and listen for decision making about how they plan time for the literacy block. I keep my eye on transition times and the children's movement from one activity to the next. Do they know where the best place might be to play alphabet games? Do they know what materials they will need and how to get them out and put them away? I'm looking for increased self-confidence because of what they are now able to do that they were unable to do previously. I look for children who know when they can do it themselves and when they need to ask for help.

The kindergarten classroom is built on the children's growing ability to be *social and cooperative*. I expect to see a change in the way children interact with others. I expect to hear more social language, "I would like a turn with the pointer, please" or "You be the dog and I'll be the lion." I listen for comments being made and questions being asked. Can I substantiate growth in individual children taking responsibility for actions and decisions? How are their relationships with other classmates? I look for a high level of enjoyment in their cooperative ventures.

And finally, I keep my eye on the development of their *work and study skills*. I note the difference in how much intervention I need to provide now, versus when I monitored this skill previously. I watch for increasing abilities to work effectively, both alone and in groups. I look for how they are able to keep track of what they are expected to do and what has been accomplished. I listen and watch for what they can now do: for example, "I need to move where it's quieter" or "I know where to find a sharp pencil" or "If I clip my painting on this clothesline, it will dry" or "I know how to spell *the*." I watch for growth in their ability to attend to what they are expected to do and do it.

DEVELOPMENTALLY APPROPRIATE PRACTICES

The International Reading Association and The National Association for the Education of Young Children (*Young Children* July 1998) have released a joint position statement on Developmentally Appropriate Practices for young children. This statement articulates the belief that "goals and expectations for young children's achievement in reading and writing should be developmentally appropriate, that is, challenging but achievable with sufficient adult support." When we understand that developmentally appropriate practices are practices that are age appropriate, individually appropriate, and culturally appropriate for each student in the class (NAEYC, 1997), we understand that it is our responsibility to meet a diverse range of individual differences. For more information on Developmentally Appropriate Practices visit the website of the National Association for the Education of Young Children. www.naeyc.org

---

My expectations are not that children will have these essential skills mastered. I know that as children's literacy skills develop at different times and in different ways, so will the essential skills develop to different degrees and different rates. But by observing children during independent work with those skills in mind, I can more effectively support the development of the whole child.

This chapter has addressed the development of knowledge and skills in the emergent reader through descriptions of how time is used in small group and individual instruction. It has also addressed time used to develop the Essential Skills as children consolidate their learning. Chapter 9 focuses on the shift I must make in my support, as children move beyond the emergent stage to the early stage of development.

9 developing the knowledge and skills of the early learner

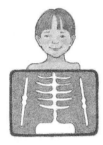

A shift from the emergent stage of literacy to the early stage of literacy does not happen in one day. During the transition, characteristics of both stages of development can be observed in any one student. Teachers look for behaviors that indicate a transition is occurring. The attitudes, knowledge, and skills identified on The Literacy Record are evidence of progress along the literacy continuum. Margaret Mooney's Characteristics of Learners (2004) descriptions of emergent and early learners are particularly helpful (see Appendix C). By understanding the key benchmarks of the literacy continuum, teachers anticipate a student's development along it. Moving ahead of the students, looking for what they can almost do independently, a teacher can be ready to support their learning when they are unable to take the next step without support.

What are some of the indications of a shift along the continuum of learning, and how can they be identified? Listening to what students say is one way. I listen to the way they respond to what others are saying, the way they ask questions, and how they make appropriate comments. I observe them in the whole group as they question, comment or respond. In small group instruction, I listen to the opinions they express and the way knowledge is shared without prompting. And finally I note any increase in the competence and confidence they develop as they talk about their writing in table conversation with others.

When students are writing every day, planning sketches begin to include more recognizable information. Bodies appear on people who previously had legs coming out of their heads. Progressive thoughts are evident when a plan about a trip to the park includes the swings and slide as well as the two people who went to play. Information is presented more clearly as writing skills develop.

Teachers should note how children use what they know as readers in their writing and what they know as writers in their reading, observing them anticipate what the writer wants them to do when they read, and what the reader will think when they write. What students know about letters and sounds supports predictions at the word level when they read. Students use what they know about hearing sounds and about letter clusters, endings, and words to record what they want to say in writing. Knowing what students do keeps the teacher's eye on what they need to learn next.

HOW MY CLASSROOM HAS CHANGED IN SEVEN MONTHS

The walls look different from the beginning of the year. On one wall are stories from our trip to the zoo. Each reflects an experience the students considered important. I think about why this group of children seemed to gain so much from this experience. I reflect upon our conversations prior to the trip, and how the students were encouraged to look for answers to their animal questions during the visit. Cardboard clipboards and index cards allowed them to bring sketches back to remember what they had seen. A piece of writing from Marcy (Figure 9.1) prior to the zoo trip confirms my thinking.

I look at the variety of published work on the walls. The group has kept me on my toes, thinking about different ways to publish their work. The level of engagement in their writing has been directly related to their interest in having it published. I see Nina's paper-stuffed narwhale with the facts she has discovered noted on cards hanging down from it. Stories are published on chart paper with colorful illustrations large enough to be noticed. Laminated story cards are hung from clothespins and yarn along one wall reflecting another choice in publication. Carlos' poster, "How to Use the Computer," reflects a new enthusiasm in his writing.

The zoo trip confirms the students' interest in living things. They have had earlier access to expository texts than classes in previous years, and I see the impact this has had on their reading, writing, and content vocabulary. Their natural interest in living things around them has encouraged meaningful questions. I find informational books in the discovery space often, a sign the children know where to look for answers to their questions.

The attention I gave to establishing and monitoring the routines for the classroom now has its benefits. I rarely have to intervene in the morning routine. The

I want to go to

the zoo because

I want to see

the cheetah

because I

am researching

on a cheetah.

Figure 9.1: Marcy's Writing Seven Months into the School Year

children are secure in knowing that each morning begins the same way, and that they are expected to be responsible for the same things.

SHIFTING SUPPORT TO SCAFFOLD LEARNING

A shift in the teacher's support occurs as children begin to acquire more literacy knowledge and become more skillful in speaking, reading, and writing. Students assume more responsibility for using their new skills also. Instruction still has the intimacy, support, and conversational nature that characterizes the emergent stage of development, but my students now are expected to work with more independence.

In small group instruction, I expect most children to match word-by-word when reading and need little support from me. I expect students to predict as a matter of course, and I listen rather than prompt. I expect they will use pictures to confirm what they have read. The students often respond now in anticipation of my question, "What made you say that?"

I can read what the children write because I know more about them. The need to publish alongside them each day is no longer necessary; now I can read the work later and determine the support that I need to provide for their next learning step.

My support can be planned. A word, a moment with a child, a short instructional episode with two or three students and I can often make a big difference to small things that have become challenges.

Figure 9.2 illustrates my daily plan seven months into the year. Note the difference from the beginning of the year. Note that now more instruction occurs in small groups rather than with individuals, as it did in the early part of the school year. I also expect more independent work and more of my time is spent monitoring individual students. I approach instruction differently as well.

Whole Group Demonstration

As this day begins, children filter into the classroom. They now know what to do. Their daily planning sheets are in the middle of each table for easy access. They begin planning their literacy time. This time allows me a few minutes to talk with parents about their children. I attend to the daily paperwork: attendance, notes from home, lunch count. I also keep an eye out for those students who still need help planning their day.

Reading and writing demonstrations occur together at the beginning of the day. The objective for my reading demonstration is how to use text features (photos and diagrams) to answer their own questions.

Because of our interest in living things and because it is part of the kindergarten curriculum, the focus of the classroom is on the plants, animals, and fish living in the discovery space of the classroom. My demonstration uses informational text with the objective of linking the questions we ask to the places we can find information in the text. Most of the available texts are too challenging for my students to read independently. I know they are keen observers of photographs and drawings. With support, they will learn to use text features to answer their questions. My demonstration is about modeling the kinds of questions they can ask themselves as readers.

I look for the way the demonstration elicits different responses from different children. Some may talk about the text features in a different way. Some may use information in their writing. Others may choose to draw or paint what they have learned while some could use the storytelling area to demonstrate what they now know.

DAILY PLAN

WRITING DEMONSTRATION	READING DEMONSTRATION	SONGS/POETRY
Obj: Use of plan to sustain writing over a number of days. Topic: Dishwasher Soap	Obj: using photographs to answer questions in non-fiction text Text: Care of your Guinea Pig	Brush your teeth (ch) Down by the Bay (rhyme)

Small Group Instruction

READING	READING	WRITING	WRITING
Obj: Attending to detail to uncover deeper meaning Group: Marcy, Quenton, Anna, Jaren Resource: My Dog Fuzzy	Obj: using initial letter to predict Group: Celia, Kyle, Jasmine Resource: I was Walking	Obj: Too revise by adding on Group: Caleb, Jazz, Celeste Resource: Draft Book Post-its	Obj: To record & share zoo experience Group: Alberto, Sophie, Julio, Janisha Resource: Chart, Markers, Photos

Publishing

NAME	TEACHING POINT
Beau —>	spaces between words
Anna —>	adding on
Colin —>	"ing" endings

Monitoring Learning

Focus: Spelling practice
Who? Paul, Keisha

Focus: Retelling (flannel board)
Who? Charles, Maria, Keisha

Focus: Phonemic awareness/rhyme
Who? Alberto, Celia, Jasmine

Focus: Independent Reading
Who? Sophie, Kyle, Celeste

NOTES
Monitor spaces between words (Beau) 3/9

Spelling
Celia - baby, happy
Anna - me, at, cat
Jazz - they, ship, crash
Alberto - it, sit, does

Oral Reading
Sophie
Kyle
Nina

Figure 9.2: Daily Plan Seven Months into the School Year

I note what Colin has written as a persuasive piece (Figure 9.3) and how Nina responded with a piece of poetry (Figure 9.4).

I wish

that people

would stop

killing

animals

like elephants and

spotted animals and

striped animals.

Figure 9.3: Colin's Persuasive Piece

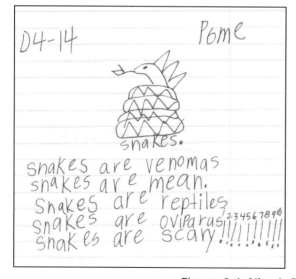

Snakes are venomous.

Snakes are mean.

Snakes are reptiles.

Snakes are oviparous.

Snakes are scary!

Figure 9.4: Nina's Poetry

In addition to using informational text, I continue to build students' understanding about how language works through the use of poetry, songs, rhyme, and rhythm. As the children begin to attend more closely to the visual information in their reading and writing, we revisit songs and poetry from the beginning of the year, now in order to focus on clusters of sounds, blends, diagraphs, and endings found in something they already know. The poetry and song charts are helpful to put words together as well as use them in sentences and lines of text.

Writing demonstrations continue to focus on developing good attitudes about daily writing. Many children have written a new piece each day since the beginning of the year. Now I want them to see how writers can continue their writing over more than one day.

My past demonstrations have modeled plans with two parts. I use the plan to "remember" what I need to write about when I write tomorrow. The example below shows what it sounds like when I talk aloud about using my plan.

"I'd better re-read what I have written so far, so I know where to start. Let's see. Those check marks in the first two boxes remind me that I have already written about these two parts of the story. I want to make sure I haven't left anything important out." I read, then make some changes to my writing and check the third of the four boxes of my plan.

While the plan is the focus for my demonstration, I also talk about words and how language sounds when words are put together. For example: "Darn! I forgot to get dishwasher soap at the store. I have an idea. I'll use laundry soap. That will work. After all, soap is soap, right?" I stop and smile. "I like how that sounds... soap is soap, right?"

I know a major predictor for reading success is the vocabulary my children continue to develop. What I read and what I write are often selected because the content vocabulary offers new language to be explored and learned.

I see the children anticipate what will happen next as they read. I add phrases to my writing that show how writers want their readers to anticipate and that they have to plan their writing to build anticipation. One of my goals is to continually heighten their awareness of how reading impacts writing and writing impacts reading.

Working with Small Groups

Small Group Reading Instruction

I plan my instruction with the expectation that my students have a good understanding of directionality, word-by-word matching, and a bank of words they can recognize and use. They can read some books independently. They predict page by page, but I notice some children do not use pictures and the text together to make sense of the book as a whole. The objective for these children is to learn how to attend to details in the picture and text to uncover deeper meaning.

The early stage of reading requires the careful selection of appropriate books for instruction (see Mooney 2004a). I look for texts that provoke thinking. Many beginning books for young readers are label books or pattern books that offer little to stimulate the kinds of conversations the students are becoming used to. These books overemphasize print features and minimize meaning. I look for a book containing enough information both in the text and the illustrations to allow children to work at clarifying the meaning of the story.

Figure 9.5: Cover of *My Dog Fuzzy*

Figure 9.6: Close Match between Picture and Text in *My Dog Fuzzy*

me!

8

Figure 9.6: Close Match between Picture and Text in *My Dog Fuzzy* *(continued)*

For my reading group today, I have selected the text *My Dog Fuzzy* (see Figure 9.5) (Boland 2001) because of the supports it provides. The topic of the book is appealing; it's about a pet. The characters are familiar: mom, dad, brother, sister, and friends.

The text, shown in Figure 9.6, has a predictable pattern with a change at the end of each line to provide a positive challenge for the reader: *Fuzzy ran past my* _____. The children can use the illustrations to predict the pattern change, but they will need to check their predictions against the visual information they get from the text. The text is in a natural language that matches the way children might talk.

The content in the illustrations is a close match to the print on each page. At the same time, the illustrations offer a challenge. There is an object in each illustration that leads us to the plot of the story; the dog continues to run despite the fact that each illustration has appealing distractions to most dogs.

Punctuation poses a challenge on the final two pages. The text allows children to predict "What might happen next?" and confirm "I thought that's what would happen" on each page until the last two pages. Note that the ellipse on the next to the last page could cause the reader to pause and wonder in the middle of the sentence: *Fuzzy ran to ....* Then the last page is a surprise, which uncovers the reason that the dog was running past the temptations.

Because the children can do more of the reading work independently in this early stage of reading development, I take the opportunity to jot a few monitoring notes. I know what I'm looking for. I note whose eyes attend to the print. I see whose fingers are moving underneath the print, I look for facial expressions that indicate understanding or confusion, and I listen for comments that inform me about what is going on inside their heads. I hear questions from the students also such as, "I wonder what will happen next?" I ask questions and have suggestions of my own, "How do you know that? Turn to the person next to you and tell them what you're thinking. Let's read the next two pages and see what happens."

We might begin our group as follows:

Each child takes a book from a pile in the middle of the circle and looks at the cover and the title. I hear them reading the title.

Quenton: My Dog.... Fluffy.

Jaren: My Dog...Fuzzy.

I comment, "I heard Fluffy and Fuzzy. I wonder what it might be."

Anna: It's got to be Fuzzy because it has two z's.

"Does everyone agree?" I ask. The children nod.

Marcy: This book is about a dog, of course.

I interject, "The title is My Dog Fuzzy. I'm wondering about that word *My*. What does that make you think?"

Quenton: It belongs to someone, probably a kid.

I wonder, "Have you ever had a pet that you could call my pet? My dog, my cat, my hamster?"

Jaren: I have a dog, well it's everyone in my family's dog but it likes me so much that it sleeps with me.

Anna: I always wanted my dog to sleep with me but my Mom says he's too big.

Marcy: I had a cat once and it used to meow and meow if I didn't let it in my room.

Jaren: My gerbil used to bite my dad but he didn't bite me.

I ask the group, "So is there anything you're wondering?" I wait for awhile, but there's no response. I continue, "Well, I'm wondering who this dog Fuzzy belongs to. Who does he like best? Let's look at the title page," I say. "Have you found more information?"

Nina: I think he's running. His feet are up in the air.

Jaren: Me too!

I ask, "What does it make you wonder?"

Jaren: I wonder why he's running.

Marcy: I wonder where he's going.

There may be pages that some children can read quietly. Because children can become dependent upon the oral reading or subvocalization of others, I begin to encourage "reading inside your head." I encourage them to move from subvocalization to reading quietly. Short periods for silent reading let me observe how they manage that task on their own.

I suggest, "Why don't you go ahead and read the first page very quietly."

The children read, some silently, some very softly. The text says, *Fuzzy ran past my mom.*

"What did you find out?" I ask.

Quenton: Fuzzy ran past the mom and on this page he ran past the dad on this page.

The children's comments confirm my expectation. Because they are accustomed to the pattern of language in the text, they are forgetting to take in some of the details that will provide the deeper meaning. I probe a bit further.

"Hmm...," I remark. "It sounds like this book is pretty easy for you to read, but I'm wondering if we might need to slow down and think a bit. You had two questions before we started reading." I record on a small chart "Why is Fuzzy running? Where is he going?" I continue, "We might need to be looking for more information to find out the answers to those questions."

Anna: Look at the picture. The mom is cooking and he's running. Maybe she's yelling at him.

"Could be," I comment. "Your idea to look at the picture is a good one, Nina. Let's all do that."

Jaren: Fuzzy—it's on his dog dish. Why would he run past his dog dish?

The group looks at the next page and continues to talk, wondering why Fuzzy would ignore the slipper and the newspaper. There's quite a discussion about things dogs like.

I listen to the conversation as closely as I listen to the words being read. My role is to support meaning making, supporting the child's developing skill in anticipating, approximating, and self-correcting. This support shifts the emphasis from the idea that reading is "getting all the words right" to gaining meaning from the text.

I want readers who are thinkers and problem solvers; I want the children to shift attention beyond what they currently know to what they need to know next. With early readers, I give support where it is needed. The entry point for instruction is having students think about a deeper meaning in this text.

The children read the next two pages, commenting before they read about the temptations that a dog might have, with the bone and the baseball. They are beginning to anticipate who the dog is running toward through their conversation.

Marcy: I saw a dog run fast to get to some other dogs.

Jaren: That happens at my apartment. They have dog time in the afternoon and everybody takes their dog outside. My dog knows when it's dog time and gets really excited.

I say, "Keep reading. Read page 6 to yourselves, then stop."

Feedback from the reading group allows me to give support where there is a challenge they do not yet have the skills to overcome. I can do this by segmenting the text into pages or sections that enable me to watch and listen carefully to allow me to anticipate the challenges children may meet and the instruction that can then occur. I make instructional decisions designed to solidify and extend the learning of these children.

They are beginning to catch on. I encourage them to keep on thinking. I suggest, "Let's go back and think about what Fuzzy has done so far. Who has he been running past?" The children quickly recount where he's been—past mom, dad, sister, brother, friends—and a few remark that he ran past a tree, while looking at page 7. "I notice that you're looking at page 7. Let's go ahead and read it, but don't turn the page yet," I say. I watch to see what these children do with the ellipse at the end of the line: Fuzzy ran to...

The children look a bit puzzled, so I ask, "I wonder what those three dots are?"

Quenton: Tree! They want you to fill in the word—t-r-e!

"Good thinking! We'd better check, so let's read it that way," I suggest. We all read together, "Fuzzy ran to tree."

Marcy: They forgot the word the.

"That's good thinking, too. Actually those three dots are there because the author wants to send you a message," I tell the children. "She's asking you to slow down your reading and think."

I have explained the purpose of the ellipse and how it is part of a bigger idea of this book, anticipating a conclusion on the last page

"So if the author wants us to think, let's read that page together and see what happens when we slow down," I say.
We read, "Fuzzy ran to..."

The children begin to anticipate, *"the grandma," "the school," "the store..."*

"Ah," I continue, "What that author wanted us to do with those three dots really worked. We're wondering where Fuzzy is going next. Turn the page and find out!"

"me!"

The children read and laugh!

Quenton: OHhhh... I get it now. (He turns to the beginning of the book.) *That's where he was going all this time!*

Because each moment of the kindergarten day is a learning moment, I have to gather information on the run. I have different kinds of questions I ask at this early continuum stage as I observe and monitor the students:

- How well does the child use prior knowledge to interact with the text? Marcy says, *"I saw a dog run fast to get to some other dogs."* Jaren responds, *"That happens at my apartment. They have dog time in the afternoon and everybody takes their dog outside. My dog knows when it's dog time and gets really excited."*
- Does the child pay particular attention to visual information? Does the child attend to phrases, words, and letters? Marcy says, *"They forgot the word* the.*"*
- Does the child look purposefully for more information? Does the child search? Anna says, *"It's got to be* Fuzzy *because it has two z's."*
- Is the child able to predict alternatives or probabilities of the text on the basis of what they know or what they learn while reading? Does the child anticipate words, language structure, and meaning? Quenton says, *"Fuzzy ran to... tree!* t-r-e.*"*

- Is the child able to reconsider a response against more than one source of information? Does the child check letter sounds, language structure, and meaning? Marcy says, *"They forgot the word* the.*"*
- Is the child able to accept the appropriateness of a response? Does the child confirm or reject? The children read the next two pages, commenting before they read on the temptations that a dog might have, with the bone and the baseball. They are beginning to anticipate who the dog is running to through their conversation.
- Is the child able to provide an accurate response in light of new information? Does the child self-correct? Quenton comments, *"OHhhh... I get it now. That's where he was going all this time!"*

My notes of observations will help me plan the next piece of instruction for each student. Some may remain with this group or I may regroup.

Small Group Writing Instruction

Revision of writing for young children begins early in the year, as I rove the room while they write. For these early writers, revision is often adding ideas to expand the meaning being created. The child who writes, "I went to the circus," as in Figure 9.7, might be asked questions like, "So you went to the circus? What did you see there?" The child's oral response to these questions provides the basis for adding on. I listen to those oral responses and suggest to the child, "Write that down. I'll be back." Going back to hear how the writing has changed instills in the child the sense of audience.

Revision begins when children are regularly asked questions. They begin to see how writers help each other. Throughout the kindergarten year, I group together students who can help each other this way. In these informal groups, students have learned the questions that writers need to ask of themselves and that can be asked of others.

Students who need daily instruction through publishing become fewer as they understand how writers write, how they control more sounds, and have a bank of words they can use. Some children will need individual support to get them started, a word or two of encouragement as I pass, and some will be grouped together and work with me.

The important thing about revision is that students learn to make sense of their writing and understand that their writing will change. Here's how a writing conference might sound:

I went to the circus. It was fun. We had to do the Star Spangled Banner. The End. I get to see a man doing a hand stand on a stick. The end. And I saw an elephant and a horse. Also tigers and more. The end.

Figure 9.7: Revising by Adding On

I begin by saying, "You each have a piece of writing that you want to share. What do we do when we come to a revision conference?"

Children: We put our draft book behind us.

We need to listen to the person who is reading their story.

We need to think if we have questions.

We need to look at the writer when we ask questions.

I ask, "What about the person reading their piece?"

Child: We need to be able to hear them!

These expectations not only support the writers reading their own writing but also encourage the development of the others as listeners, speakers, and viewers.

I ask, "Who's ready?" All of the children volunteer. I select Caleb.

Caleb reads (see Figure 9.8): "I got a stubbed toe. It really ached. Yeow!"

Figure 9.8: Caleb's Writing

Conversation occurs about other experiences with stubbing toes.

Celeste asks, "How did it happen?"

Caleb replies, "I was playing in the yard."

Jazz asks, "But what did you do?"

Caleb replies, "Look here (he points to his plan). See? I was wearing bare feet."

Celeste says, "You ought to put that in your story."

"So Caleb, what are you going to do?" I ask.

Caleb: "I'm going to add the part about bare feet. That's how I stubbed my toe."

Caleb adds the part about his bare feet to the end of his piece, shown in Figure 9.9.

Our questions help writers ask themselves the same questions. My goal is that these questions be as much part of writing as the planning of ideas. What will my readers want to know? What will they be wondering? Figure 9.10 indicates the writer is thinking about his reader as he writes.

Jazz reads his piece, "Once a truck went in my back yard." He asks himself what his readers will wonder and his thoughts go immediately to his parents. *"Probably my Dad and Mom said, 'Aaaaaa and Oh my gosh!'"* Then he anticipates again what his readers will want to know. He even asks and answers the question in his piece, *"Do you wonder why? Yes. Okay. The man fell asleep, OK? OK."*

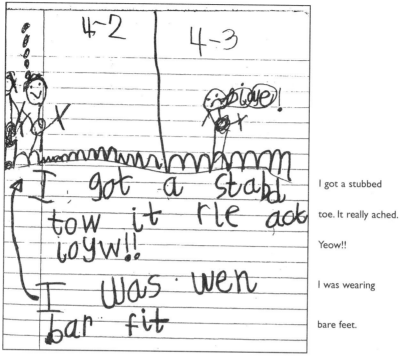

I got a stubbed

toe. It really ached.

Yeow!!

I was wearing

bare feet.

Figure 9.9: Caleb's Revised Writing

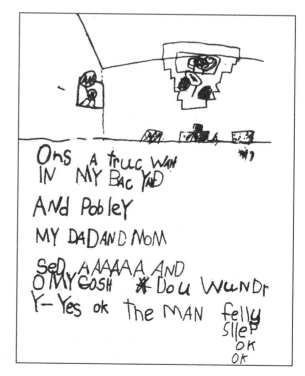

Figure 9.10: Jazz's Writing

Working with Individual Writers

Once children understand that writing is about getting ideas down on paper that someone else can read, the publication of their writing is no longer necessary each day. My support comes through listening and talking as they plan. The single sketch becomes a two-part sketch, a three-part sketch, and so on (Figure 9.11).

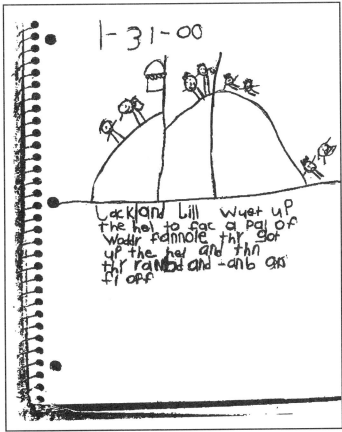

Jack and Jill went up the hill to fetch a pail of water. Finally they got up the hill and then they ran down and fell off.

Figure 9.11: Child's 3-Part Plan and Writing

Quenton has seen me demonstrate a multi-part plan. He tried a six-part plan for his narrative about a dinosaur (Figure 9.12): *"One day a little dinosaur named Ester ran away from his house and he adventured off. On the way he saw a volcano blocking the way. He had to run up the volcano before it erupted so he ran up it as fast as he could and as he ran down—BOOM! It erupted but Ester made it right before it erupted. After that he snuck into..."*

Instruction in Leaving Spaces Between Words

Moving into the early stage of the literacy continuum means children are beginning to hear more than just the initial sounds in words. Those essential words, such as *I, to, is, me,* and *my,* are also used more consistently in their writing. Hearing more sounds in words and having knowledge of essential words indicates that children are ready for instruction in how to leave spaces between words. Here is how I work with Beau to help him understand that there are spaces between words.

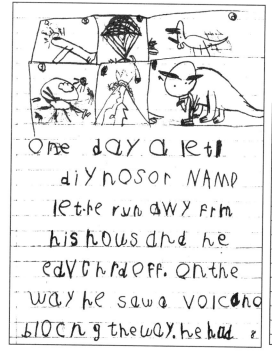

Figure 9.12: Quenton's Multi-Part Plan and Writing

I ask Beau to read his writing. He proceeds with some difficulty (see Figure 9.13).

I say, "I'm going to teach you something that will make it easier for you to read your own writing. You're going to learn to leave spaces between words. Let's find the first word in your story." I am confirming that Beau knows the difference between a letter and a word when I ask that question. Beau points to *I.* I say, "Write the word *I* under your sentence." Beau writes the word. "What's the next word?" I ask.

Figure 9.13: Beau Revising His Writing to Include Spaces between Words

Beau says, "Been."

"Now think about where *been* will go if you leave a space. Show me where you would start," I continue. Beau points, leaving a space. "Good! Go ahead and write it." He does.

We continue in the same way writing the next few words. Beau has written, *I been sick for...*

I note at the bottom of my teaching plan to monitor Beau for the next few days to see if he leaves spaces between words in writing, and if he notices them in reading. At each opportunity, I gently nudge him toward independence. Beau may need to be reminded about spaces between words several times. I am careful to keep my distance and be encouraging, yet I ensure that he understands what he has to learn and that he uses his new learning.

A Note on Phonics and Spelling

As children develop as writers, they learn more about print features such as phonics and spelling. Once students have a bank of ten to fifteen essential words and begin to make sound-to-letter links, they are on the way to developing phonics and spelling skills.

Phonics teaching has traditionally been the teaching of letters and the associated sound the voice makes to represent those letters, matching the letter to the

PHONICS

Definition: The relationship between the letters of written language and the sounds of spoken language (NCLB).

What do we need to know?

Research has shown us that readers use multiple sources of information when they read (Rumelhart 1994). One source of information, the visual source of information includes phonics. In the ongoing debate about quality reading instruction, there has been a tendency to look at programs to teach reading (Chall 1983). In the past, reading programs, or methodologies, have either emphasized phonics instruction or ignored it. Thus instructional methods for reading have become polarized—for phonics or against phonics. Knowledgeable, skillful teachers understand that readers need to understand the relationship between sounds and letters, just as they need to understand the syntax involved in reading and understanding that reading must make sense.

Interestingly, the debate has not often included the reciprocal nature of reading and writing. Skillful teachers understand that writers must know how to hear and record sounds in the words they write, making writing an excellent vehicle for phonics instruction.

Assessment Tools

Observations of learners while reading and writing allow the teacher to see how the readers and writers are using what they know about phonics. The oral reading record provides evidence that allows the teacher to analyze all sources of information, including phonics. Systematic analysis of student writing allows the teacher to see what the writer knows about recording sounds and phonetic generalizations. Comparing the reading and writing assessments from the same learner consistently allows the teacher to evaluate the ability to apply what is known in reading to writing and what is known in writing to reading.

(Adapted from *Literacy Learning: Teachers as Professional Decision Makers Resource Book*, Katonah, NY: Richard C. Owen, 2004.)

sound. Typically phonics was taught in isolation with the class "doing" the same letter at the same time, whether or not some children knew the letter. Instruction was delivered by a phonics program relying on isolated instruction of sounds. What the teacher did was determined by a program. Phonics was taught through programs that turned letters into people and where celebrations were held to marry q and u. The program drove the practice rather than the practice being driven by student's need.

Children do need direct and systematic phonics instruction, but this instruction occurs one-to-one through publishing student writing or in small group instruction when children have similar needs.

The important thing is to assess, record, and ensure that every student in the class receives instruction where and when they need it. Organizing the classroom and managing learning opportunities are especially important and ensures this can happen.

Monitoring individual student growth ensures that a system is in place for each child. I record the letters and sounds the student knows. I note the sounds and letters the student currently uses when writing. Running records and notes indicate how effectively students use letters and sounds when reading.

Approximations are a young learner's way of saying, "Here is what I know about this word." Those approximations that are one or two letters away from accuracy can usually be corrected with a few minutes of direct instruction. As children begin to understand sound-to-letter correspondence, their approximations become closer and closer to conventional spelling.

Close approximations of spelling need to be corrected as they appear. Otherwise they persist as inaccuracies. How many teachers of older learners are challenged by students who spell the word they, *t-h-a-y,* after years of spelling the word incorrectly? What would have happened if the teacher had taught the correct spelling of the word the first time this approximation was noted?

Example of Instruction in Spelling Practice

Writing instruction begins with an evaluation of the writer's strengths. I consider the writer's use of both process and surface features. An evaluation of Anna's writing is shown in Figure 9.14.

Anna has good ideas for a young writer. As she gains more control over the surface features of writing, she can deal with more ideas; the more words she can write, the more ideas she'll express.

She knows how to spell the words *my, I,* and *a*. She closely approximates the words *me* and *cat.* Those two words she will use both as a reader and a writer,

PROCESS FEATURES		SURFACE FEATURES
STRENGTHS: Selects topic of importance Sketch includes a speech balloon with cat saying, "Take me for a walk." Express ideas clearly. Uses dialogue, complex thought, and humor in draft. Has logical conclusion.		**STRENGTHS:** Punctuation—Period at the end of piece Spelling: Correct spelling of *my, I, a* Identifies beginning and ending sounds in words and often records both (*kt/cat, sd/said, wk/walk*). Grammar: Uses dialogue appropriately.

Figure 9.14: Anna's Plan and Writing

since she and her cat are her most frequent topic selections for writing. Her use of the word *cat* provides the opportunity to introduce her to the word at. She can then make links to a number of other words as she writes. Too many new words at once can be confusing. I begin with what she already knows and decide from there. A spelling episode with Anna proceeds as follows:

I begin, "You and I have talked about how great this piece of writing is. I still laugh when I read the part where the cat is telling you to take it for a walk. That was a clever way to tell that part of your story."

Anna smiles, "My dad thought it was funny too!" She had told her family about her story the night before.

"Today we're going to work on a few new words that will help you write more easily. Let's look at your draft book. Can you reread your story and I will tell you when to stop."

Anna reads, "My cat said to me..."

"Stop at that word me and take a closer look at it." I point to my. "Is there anything you notice?"

Anna responds, "It says my... Oops!"

Before I can ask another question, she draws a line through my and writes the word me.

I encourage children to line out words rather than erase in their draft books. Lining out allows me to see the thinking that was going on when the child was drafting. I have useful information about what was corrected and why.

"Good for you. What does it say now?" I ask.

"Me!" Anna replies.

Anna's actions confirm what I suspected. She already knew the word *me* and just needed a reminder to look more carefully. She saw that it did not "look right." This tells me that she is able to take on a few new words.

"I'm going to put that word on your list of words to practice. It will be an easy one for you to remember. This is another word you need to know. It's the little word *at*. It only has two letters. I write two lines on her draft book page: _ _.

Anna says, "I know it has a 't' in it."

"Where do you think that might go?" I ask.

She points to the second line. I hand her my pen, and she writes it. "The first letter in that word is *a*," I tell her. "Why don't you write that on the first line?"

She writes the letter *a*. "So how do you spell that word *at*?" I ask.

"a-t," she replies.

"Look at it really closely and try to remember how it looks. Can you close your eyes and see that word?" I ask. "What letters do you see?"

"a-t," she replies.

I continue, "Open your eyes. If I cover the word *at* in your draft book, will you be able to write it?"

I cover the word and she quickly writes *a-t.*

I ask her, "Does it look right?" and she quickly answers yes.

"The great thing about knowing that word *at* is how much it will help you when you are spelling something like *cat*. If you know at then you just have to say to yourself, 'What would I put at the beginning of *at* to make it *cat*?' "

Anna says, "k?"

I provide a little more support, "There are two letters that make the sound you hear at the beginning of cat."

SPELLING NOTEBOOK

Children need to learn how to practice spelling words. The procedure for practicing is as follows: Practicing spelling words becomes an independent daily activity. The spelling notebook is a record of known vocabulary for both reading and writing. The words included in the notebook have meaning and purpose for the child. They are accessible to the child and are the child's own words. The spelling notebook becomes a personalized word wall for each child. An individualized spelling notebook enables me to carefully monitor the child's learning of new words and how they use them in their writing. In the back of the spelling notebook is a grid for me to record the new words each week.

She immediately says, "Oh, I remember. c—it's on my alphabet card with a picture of a cat!"

"I thought you knew that," I reply. "Let's put the words *me, at,* and *cat* in your spelling notebook so you can practice them until you know them." I write the words in Anna's spelling notebook: *me, at, cat*

My objective is not only to teach Anna a new word, but to support her in a strategy for practicing words and to remember how they look. Gaining mastery of words, knowing what they look like as they are read requires practice. Students need time to practice in the classroom so I can observe them.

Spelling is visual. Spellers use all they know about how words work to spell the word, but the final check allows them to ask, "Does it look right?" and the way it is practiced will support the writer in answering that question.

OBSERVING AND MONITORING LEARNING BEHAVIOR

Throughout this book I have constantly referred to the importance of the observation and recording of learning behavior as a marker of development along a learning continuum. With any class of students, so much is going on it's easy to forget or overlook what one or another child did when the teacher's attention is not consistently focused upon learning and making a record of it. Too often, I imagine, teachers feel they are not doing their job unless they are "teaching," which often means presenting to their students, rather than observing them and

Spelling Practice

1. **Look** at the word and /say/ the word.

2. **Close** your eyes and (**picture**) the word.

3. **Cover** the word.

4. **Write** the word.

check ✓
5. **Check** the word.

listening to what they have to say. In my definition, teaching is as much the observation of what students learn to do or practice by themselves as it is the direct instruction they receive from the teacher.

If we were to analyze the activity of teaching by what I have advocated in the preceding chapters, we would determine that teaching has four key components. They include the kinds of instruction given in the whole class group. I have usually referred to this as demonstration. Then there is the instruction offered in small groups that is as varied as the content and needs of the students. There is also the instruction, formal and informal, that meets the special needs of individual students. But most important of all is *where* the instruction itself begins: from knowing where each student is, knowing what he or she knows and understands from the observation and monitoring of their learning that is a constant in the life of a teacher. It's easy to say how much time should be spent on this important component of teaching—every moment of the teaching day!

There are certain ways I gather information about learning while students work independently in different areas of the classroom. Roving is moving around the room and monitoring learning. It is something that the teacher does intentionally. I know which student I'm going to see and what I'm looking for. Every rove has a purpose.

In a Classroom Library Space

I can observe growth in communication skills as I watch children read and listen to conversations about books in the classroom library space. I hear some students beginning to express opinions and discriminate about their book selection. I note their ability to make choices and manage time while in the library workspace.

In an Art Space

Problem solving occurs in every aspect of a student's work. As I observe the art space, I see how they decide the components of their pictures, what materials they will use, and their decisions about how they will organize the size, shape, textures, and colors in their pictures. I get a window into how children think who are less likely to respond in class.

In a Rhythm and Rhyme Space

In the space where we have familiar poems, songs, and rhymes, I can observe the development of social and cooperative skills. I watch how group decisions are made about the poem to be read, who holds the pointer, and where they should stand when reciting. I also listen for word play.

In an Independent Spelling Space

Work and study skills are revealed when students work independently to practice words they are learning to spell. I note how effectively children use the spelling procedure to learn new words. I also observe how effectively they practice handwriting. I use this area to monitor the child's ability to accurately form letters.

In a Storytelling Space

Social and cooperative skills are important learning for children acting out stories they have read or written. I watch students in the storytelling space as they decide which puppets or which dress-ups will work specifically for the story they want to recreate. I watch for the initiative they take in deciding how to present in front of others. Children are able to express the meaning they make in a variety of ways. As the famous dancer Isadora Duncan once said, "If I could tell you what I mean, there would be no point in dancing" (1928).

The time spent roving and monitoring provides me with specific information about where individual students are. What do they know? What do they need to learn next? Just as importantly, this information is the key to personal reflection. It provides evidence of the impact of my instruction—the kind of teacher I am.

10   teacher reflection: thinking about our work

Celia, Julio, and Nina are children from the classroom presented in this book. They were introduced in Chapter 3 with the data from their initial assessments, and we have followed their development. In this chapter, we look at the evidence of their progress in literacy. We examine the growth they have made and why they have made it.

CELIA

Celia's growth at the beginning of the year was more evident in her spoken language than it was in her writing. The writing in Figure 10.1 after two months in school shows a shift from scribbles to random strings of letters and numbers. It shows planning with a lot of detail.

Because she is a new learner of English, the teaching focused on the development of her oral language as well as her reading and writing. By the fifth month of school, Celia had made significant progress through the emergent stage of development. She began to make a leap by recording the sounds she hears in words (Figure 10.2).

She made quick progress once she began to acquire a bank of known words and understand how recording sounds worked. At the same time, her expressive language in English was much more comprehensible. Her writing developed as she wrote about topics of great importance to her and was able to use what she knows about words and sounds (Figure 10.3).

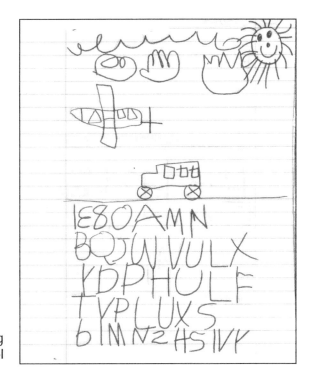

Figure 10.1: Celia's Writing after Two Months in School

Figure 10.2: I saw a train.

Figure 10.3: I am happy my mom had my baby.

I am in T-ball

practice. I am

on the A's.

It is so fun.

We are having

so much fun!

Our team

will have

a game in 10

weeks. My

grandma will come.

Figure 10.4: Celia's Writing after Seven Months of School

In a short time, Celia was adding more information to her pieces. Her approximations show evidence of her growing knowledge of English and her ability to take risks. Now, seven months into the school year, there is evidence of consistent growth in her oral language, written language, and reading (Figure 10.4).

The development in Celia's draft book is confirmed when the Observation Survey is re-administered. Figure 10.5 shows her progress since the beginning of the year.

Celia	August	March
Letter ID	0/54	52/54
Concepts about Print	1/24	18/24
Hearing and Recording Sounds in Words	0/37	29/37
Writing Vocabulary	0	27
Oral Reading Record	Emergent	Early 1

Figure 10.5: Celia's Progress Documented by the Observation Survey

Her current strengths are evident in the Hearing and Recording Sounds tasks (Figure 10.6).

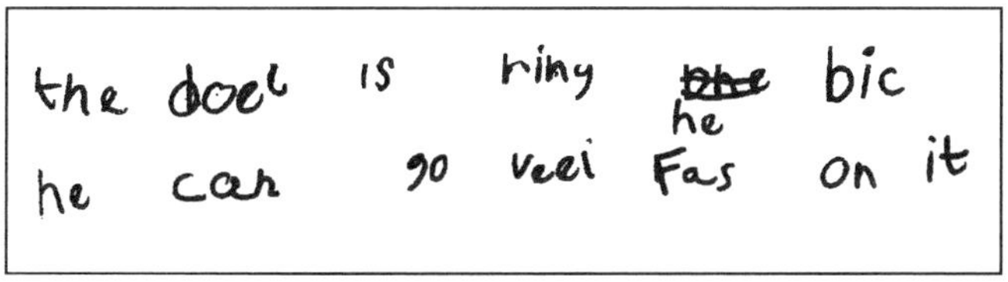

the doel is riny bic (he)
he can go veei Fas on it

The boy is riding his bike.

He can go very fast on it.

Figure 10.6: Celia's Hearing and Recording Sounds in March

Celia shows evidence of control of directionality, return sweep, and spacing between words. She has a bank of essential words: *the, is, he, can, go, on, it.* She hears initial, middle, and ending sounds in some words (*bike: b-i-c*) and shows evidence of knowledge of some endings (*riding: r-ing*).

The Writing Vocabulary task confirms her growing bank of known words (Figure 10.7). Celia made generalizations based upon what she knows (e.g., *he, she, we, man, can*).

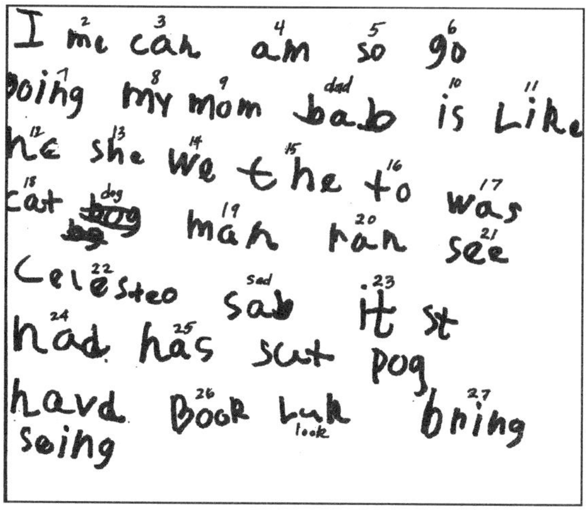

Figure 10.7: Celia's Bank of Known Words

JULIO

Julio's progress has been consistent since the beginning of the year. Once he believed he was a writer, he began to use what he knew as a reader in his writing (Figure 10.8). Note his growth by the third month of school.

I climb mountains and
the sun is almost going
dark.

Figure 10.8: Julio's Writing in the Third Month of School

Julio's work and study ethic has developed early. While animated and chatty, he's very serious about his learning and listens intently during any instructional episode. Figure 10.9 shows a current oral reading record and notes taken on his development as a reader over the past month.

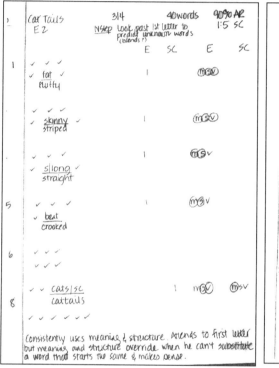

Figure 10.9 Julio's Running Record and Notes

His latest running record prompts me to look at his writing to see if he is hearing blends at the beginning of the word (Figure 10.10).

His use of blends in the words *friends: fras, play: play,* and *ever: afver* will allow him to be supported to make the link between what he knows as a writer and what he is doing as a reader.

Julio's progress is recorded through data gathered from the Observation Survey (Figure 10.11).

Most significant is his growth in writing. His confidence shows in his fluency and organization of the page in both tasks requiring him to write (Figure 10.12).

D3-6

P

me and Kyle are
fras I let him
play wif my
pawraits We are
fras for af vr.

Me and Kyle are

friends. I let him

play with my

Power Rangers. We are

friends forever.

Figure 10.10: Julio's Use of Blends in Writing

Julio	August	March
Letter ID	43/54	54/54
Concepts about Print	9/24	22/24
Hearing and Recording Sounds in Words	0/37	33/37
Writing Vocabulary	0	41
Oral Reading Record	Emergent	Early 2

Figure 10.11: Julio's Progress Documented by the Observation Survey

The B is Rtding Hes
Bak He can go vene
fast on it

go[15] see[22] in[31]
He[23] on[32]
off[33]
The[16] BeBy can[34]
a[17] my[24] cat[35]
am[18] dad[25] dog[36]
Play[26]
Can
mom[19] you[27] have[37]
man[28] be[38]
me[20] and[39]
we[21] yes[29] book[40]
no[30] look[41]

Figure 10.12: Julio's Hearing and Recording Sounds in Words and Writing Vocabulary

NINA

Nina's involvement in what she reads has changed as she has moved through the early stage of development. She expresses feelings and states opinions frequently. She automatically relates what she has read in one book to other books.

I watch for Nina to take on new learning from observing demonstrations in the classroom. When a two-part plan was demonstrated, she immediately used what she had seen in her own writing. It took a small amount of support to shift her two-part planning from caption writing to writing with more than one part (Figures 10.13 and 10.14).

Nina has developed preferences for different kinds of books and is recently interested in poetry. Making her aware of how her writing sounds like poetry generated an interest in writing poems. Her understanding of book language is evident in the poetry she writes (Figures 10.15 and 10.16).

This weekend

I hope

I get to
go to
the mall. And the park.

Figure 10.13: Nina's Two-Part Plan with Captions Under Each Picture

I like to
make cards
for my parents
because I want to
tell them how
I feel.

Figure 10.14: Nina's Two-Part Plan with an Expanded Story

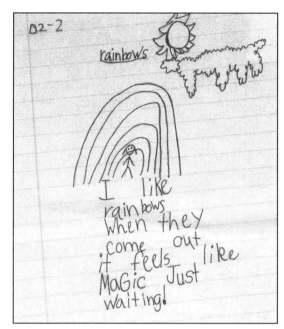

Figure 10.15: Nina's Use of Poetic Language

I like rainbows. When they come out it feels like magic just waiting!

Figure 10.16: A Poem by Nina

I got a teddy bear. I do not cry 'cause wherever I go he'll be right beside me waiting.

Yesterday I wrote
on my last page
in my old draft book
and now! I'm writing

in my new draft book.

I am proud of my-
self for finishing
a whole draft book.

Figure 10.17: Nina's Reflection on Her Own Progress

It's important to ensure Nina continues to progress to her potential. The skill lies in expanding her ability to use what she knows without losing sight of the fact that she just turned six years old (Figure 10.17).

Nina's literacy development is apparent in the recent collection of Observation Survey data (Figure 10.18).

Nina	August	March
Letter ID	52/54	54/54
Concepts about Print	18/24	24/24
Hearing and Recording Sounds in Words	35/37	37/37
Writing Vocabulary	27	70
Oral Reading Record	Early 1	Early 4

Figure 10.18: Nina's Progress Documented by the Observation Survey

IN REFLECTION

I sometimes wonder if readers will think this book paints too rosy a picture of kindergarten teaching. It is a book about what can be done with students like Celia, Julio, and Nina, and I quite deliberately overlook the tribulations, minor catastrophes, disruptions, behavioral oddities, and contrary natures that are part of a kindergarten teacher's life.

The examples I have used as "my class" in this book are real children in a real class. At the beginning of the year, nearly half of them knew less than ten alphabet letters. Well over 50% had limited concepts about print and no sound-symbol correspondence. Most had no reading or writing vocabulary, few had any preschool experiences. All this paints a rather dismal picture if we focus on only what the children are unable to do.

Focusing on strengths allows us to see the potential of very ordinary children found in any class of five and six year olds. Were there challenges with this class of children? No more and no less than with any other class. They were loud at the beginning of the school year; they talked all the time at the same time, and they all wanted to be first in line and pushed or shoved their way to get there. They called each other names and called their teacher names as well. But it didn't take long to see what they were capable of learning.

About Questions

Kindergarten teachers always have lots of questions. They often express their thoughts about the challenges of teaching kindergarten. There is no doubt that the job has its challenges. At the same time it can be one of the most enjoyable: Right in front of your eyes children grow and develop faster than any other time in school!

I think a lot about the questions and comments I hear when working with kindergarten teachers.

One said, "The children are dictating to me what they have 'written' in their draft books. In some cases the writing is phonetic. In other cases it is coming out of their heads. I 'publish' what they are dictating, in the little books."

Her students are readers, and she needs support in understanding that. Even those who are scribbling or writing with a random string of letters could be asked to put their fingers under the writing and to read what they have written. Students need to believe they are story writers, not just story tellers.

I was in a classroom where a child had been taught the word *I* several times. I could see that he was inconsistently using that word in his writing. When I asked him to put his finger under his story and read, he started with the word *I* (even though the text was mostly random stringing of letters). I mentioned that I knew he could write the word *I* and asked him to fix it. He could do it immediately. My conversation with the teacher was about what the child already knows and how the teacher might use that knowledge to develop his reading and writing further.

Another teacher asked why her students weren't more invested in their stories. Perhaps they need more time talking about what they are going to write.

Children do not always come to school with a wealth of oral language. I remember reading the original *Art of Teaching Writing* (Calkins 1986). Lucy Calkins found success with what she called "oral rehearsal." I was in a classroom once where children talked about their topics, what would be in their sketches, and what would be in their stories. They did this while eating snacks. Meanwhile, the teacher was listening and taking notes to remind herself about what they said. In another classroom, the children have a short outside break after the teacher's writing demonstration to give them time to think and talk about what they might write about. I once asked my students to sit knee to knee after a demonstration and talk about their topics and what would be in their planning sketches. Each of those experiences helped them understand that talking and writing go hand in hand.

Yet another teacher said he didn't feel as if his students were learning what they should from their writing. Obviously children are at all different places on the writing continuum coming into kindergarten. But sometimes I think we make a few giant leaps into letters and sounds with those who still need to attend to talking and drawing. The entry point for instruction may look different for the child whose illustrations are unrecognizable but whose story is about "dog." For children who haven't had that support in talking or drawing, we need to provide it in kindergarten. I think back on a child I had. When I looked at his drawing, it looked a lot like a saguaro cactus. Because I lived in Arizona at the time, I nearly asked him about his cactus. Instead I said, "Tell me about your picture." He replied, "That's me!" My instant response was, "Where's your head?" I needed to help him see that bodies needed heads, arms, legs, feet, fingers. He wasn't going to have much to write about if his drawings only looked like blobs. So I spent more time with him and others as they planned, commenting on what their drawings had and what their drawings needed. Then we talked a lot about the stories that would go with the drawings. I would tell a student that "dog" is not a story. Even the stories didn't come by themselves; they needed my support with lots of talk and lots of demonstrations of how stories work in writing.

Then, there was the teacher concerned about the publication of writing. The forms of publication can change. When books are in different shapes, or the story is published on a child-sized story cards or papers as large as a chart tablet, there would always be a new enthusiasm for writing. I remember the children in a Texas room "dramatizing" their published books. The story would be "I lost my tooth last night" and the author decided who the characters would be. Costumes were selected by the author who would be the "reader" of the story. I also remember another classroom where the teacher demonstrated publishing in front of her kids. She'd talk about color and size and texture and all the things an illustrator would need to know. If she demonstrated a new medium for publication, students were lined up to use it in their own published pieces.

And, there is often asked a question about the use of draft books at all in kindergarten, and why writing should not be kept in a folder. I can't imagine life in the classroom without a draft book (or whatever you would choose to call the house of the child's writing over time). I also can't imagine life in the classroom without published pieces, because they still are the most reliable independent reading material for emergent readers. I have seen student published books, trade books, and mimeographed books all together in a child's book bag. If I asked any of them to read me their favorite book, without exception, they each chose one they had written themselves.

Teachers who ask questions believe that the power in teaching is the power in feeling comfortable with the uncomfortable, asking questions, being satisfied with the fact that the questions might not have answers, and that there will always be more questions.

One well-known quote has always appealed to me. "We have not succeeded in answering all of our questions. In fact, we have not completely answered any of them. The answers we have found have only served to raise a whole new set of questions. In some ways we feel we are confused on a much higher level about more important things."

Values

As a teacher, I have valued being part of a professional learning environment where people are interested in what I do and ask about my practice. I value that I am asked not only what I'm doing but *why* I'm doing it.

When I was first asked that question it made me feel uncomfortable: Was what I was doing inappropriate? Was I doing something wrong? What I was doing became a question that forced me to read, talk with others, and put the "why" behind my practice. With support, I began to see changes among my students:

the intensity of their engagement, the changes in their learning behavior, and the evidence of real learning. What is more, I became aware of why I was changing my instruction. Soon I was continually asking the *why* question of myself and developing a sense of values and beliefs against which I test my practice.

I have learned to value that what I believe about teaching and learning is unshakeable. This book has been an attempt to reflect those values and beliefs. I've come to value teachers who believe learning occurs best when it is built on learner's strengths: when we determine what the learner can do, what the learner is attempting to do, and then decide what we need to do next.

In this book I have addressed this belief through the one fundamental understanding that we all have from our own experience as teachers: Children learn in different ways and at different rates. I know about the need to use quality tools to gather information, from *An Observation Survey of Early Literacy Achievement* (Clay 2002), to *My Book* (Duncan 2005), to observations of student work and observations while students work.

I have come to value teachers who believe learning is developmental: I recognize that as the more knowledgeable other we teachers develop readers, writers, mathematicians, scientists, and ourselves along a continuum. That belief is reflected in the understanding that my knowledge of child development, the language modes, what constitutes a literacy set, and a literacy continuum, all allow me to make informed judgments about the assessment data that has been collected.

I've come to value teachers who believe every learner has unlimited potential, and it is our job to realize and release that potential. In order to release that potential, I first organize my classroom into the kind of learning spaces that allows me to manage student learning. I manage my time and the students' time within the classroom environment to meet student learning needs. I provide the support for new learning to occur in whole group, small groups, and when working with individuals.

I've come to value teachers who believe personal reflection is the key to learning. Our ability to ask questions of ourselves allows us to make shifts in what we do, and why and how we do it.

Teachers' beliefs are continually being tested. Just when we think we have figured things out, we meet a new child, or read a new article, or have a conversation with a colleague that causes us to ask yet one more question. The more teachers understand, the more questions we have about what we still need to understand. The more effectively teachers gather relevant information about children, make decisions about that information, plan to manage our learning and provide instruction, the more information we have to reflect upon. It is this teacher's reflection—thinking about teaching while we are teaching—that is vital to the quality of our work.

CONCLUSION

It's a sad irony that the older a student becomes the more seriously we seem to take his or her education. The higher up the learning tree students go, the greater the prestige we seem to give their teachers. Of course college and university professors deserve our respect, yet how many of their students owe their places in a class to the opportunities they had to become readers, writers, mathematicians and thinkers as five or six year olds? Celia, Julio, and Nina are representive of any student. Parents send us the best children they have. They are, each and every one of them, the best. A kindergarten teacher's job has always been challenging and important. Teachers of five and six year olds especially deserve the commendation of every parent who attends their child's high school graduation or sees their offspring successfully launched into the independence of adult life.

Despite the great advances in knowledge, understanding, and technology, there is nothing that will replace the teacher. Nothing certainly that will replace the kindergarten teacher. That is why it is so important to be good at what we do and continually get better at it. This is where I trust *The Kindergarten Book* will be helpful.

APPENDICES

appendix a

Using My Book for Assessment

My Book is an informal assessment tool designed to assist teachers in gathering relevant data at the beginning of the kindergarten year. The assessment can be administered in a variety of ways over a number of days (see Chapter 2 of *The Kindergarten Book*). Some pages can be presented to the *whole class* for completion. Other pages will provide more information in *small groups*. You may wish to keep children in the same small groups as you complete the book to observe how they interact with each other. Some pages are more effective when administered *one on one*.

It is important to read all of the directions prior to administering the assessment so that you are familiar with the content and information you will be collecting. Note the paragraph in the letter to parents on the back of *My Book* emphasizing the book's content and that you value any attempts by the child. As you work with this tool, you should determine what best meets your needs and the needs of your students.

You can introduce the book to the whole class as a special book that will belong to them. Explain that they will be able to draw, write, and color in it because it's their own book. Share the book's text with the children, reading it aloud and inviting the children to read along. You are using this tool to gather data, so encourage the children to do the work in the book. If they do not know information such as their addresses and phone numbers, you can assist them. You need to gather as much information about each child as you can.

PAGE-BY-PAGE INSTRUCTIONS

Page	Tasks	Data Collected about the Child's Literacy Knowledge and Skills	Data Collected about the Child's Attitude toward Literacy
Contains picture of each page of *My Book*.	Lists the tasks that can be completed on each page.	Describes data about the child's literacy knowledge and skills that can be gathered on each page. Teachers may choose to gather information on some or all of these skills.	Describes data about the child's attitude toward literacy.

You can create your own form for more room for observations.

Student Name	Observations

My Book text and instructions © 2005 by Marilyn Duncan. Illustrations © 2005 by Joanne Friar. Duncan, Marilyn. *The Kindergarten Book*. Katonah, NY: Richard C. Owen Publishers, Inc., 2005.

Replacement instructions and ordering information available at our web site. Richard C. Owen Publishers, Inc. • PO Box 585 • Katonah, NY 10536 • www.RCOwen.com • Orders: 800-336-5588

Page	Tasks	Data Collected about the Child's Literacy Knowledge and Skills	Data Collected about the Child's Attitude toward Literacy
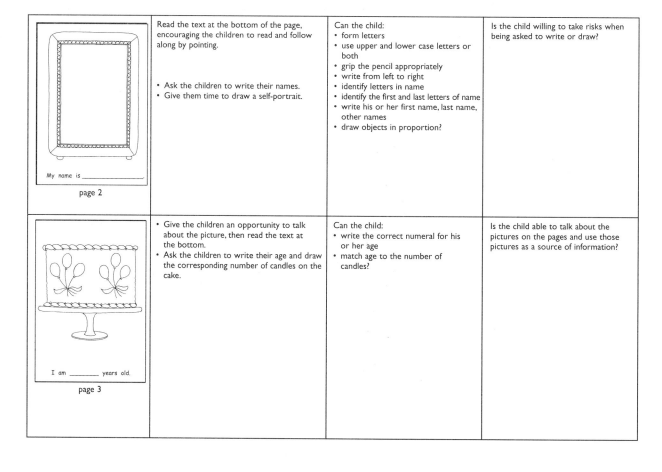 cover	Place the books in the center of a small group and ask children to take a book. Ask the children to: • find the front of the book • point to the title • read the title to the children • talk about who the book might be about.	Can the child: • identify the front of book • locate the title • articulate the content • willingly share background knowledge?	Does the child show interest in completing a book that can be taken home?
title page	Ask the children to: • turn to the title page • continue conversation with a focus on the title and content.	Can the child: • turn the pages • locate the title?	Is the child comfortable holding the book and turning the pages?
page 2	Read the text at the bottom of the page, encouraging the children to read and follow along by pointing. • Ask the children to write their names. • Give them time to draw a self-portrait.	Can the child: • form letters • use upper and lower case letters or both • grip the pencil appropriately • write from left to right • identify letters in name • identify the first and last letters of name • write his or her first name, last name, other names • draw objects in proportion?	Is the child willing to take risks when being asked to write or draw?
page 3	• Give the children an opportunity to talk about the picture, then read the text at the bottom. • Ask the children to write their age and draw the corresponding number of candles on the cake.	Can the child: • write the correct numeral for his or her age • match age to the number of candles?	Is the child able to talk about the pictures on the pages and use those pictures as a source of information?

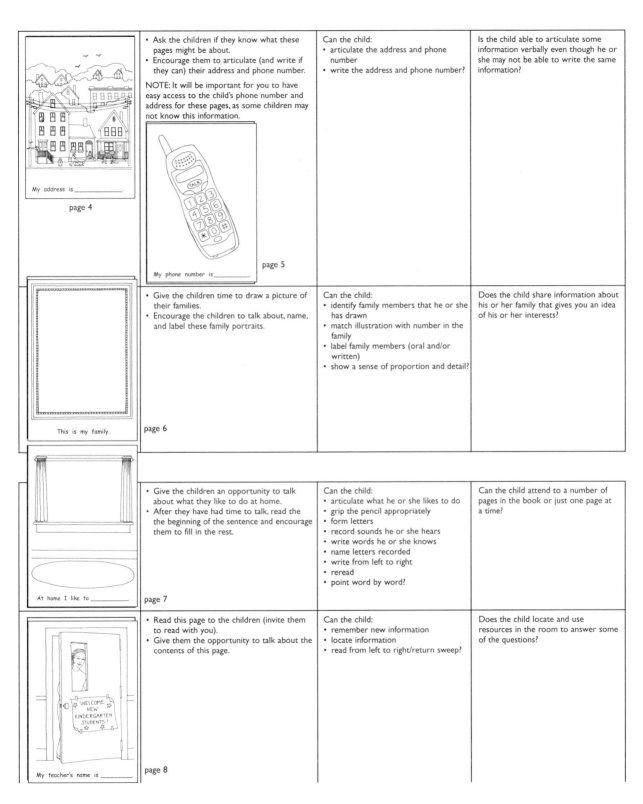

		Can the child:	Is the child able to articulate some
	• Ask the children if they know what these pages might be about. • Encourage them to articulate (and write if they can) their address and phone number. NOTE: It will be important for you to have easy access to the child's phone number and address for these pages, as some children may not know this information.	Can the child: • articulate the address and phone number • write the address and phone number?	Is the child able to articulate some information verbally even though he or she may not be able to write the same information?

My address is _____

page 4

My phone number is _____

page 5

		Can the child:	Does the child share information about
This is my family.	• Give the children time to draw a picture of their families. • Encourage the children to talk about, name, and label these family portraits.	Can the child: • identify family members that he or she has drawn • match illustration with number in the family • label family members (oral and/or written) • show a sense of proportion and detail?	Does the child share information about his or her family that gives you an idea of his or her interests?

page 6

At home I like to _____	• Give the children an opportunity to talk about what they like to do at home. • After they have had time to talk, read the the beginning of the sentence and encourage them to fill in the rest.	Can the child: • articulate what he or she likes to do • grip the pencil appropriately • form letters • record sounds he or she hears • write words he or she knows • name letters recorded • write from left to right • reread • point word by word?	Can the child attend to a number of pages in the book or just one page at a time?

page 7

WELCOME NEW KINDERGARTEN STUDENTS! My teacher's name is _____	• Read this page to the children (invite them to read with you). • Give them the opportunity to talk about the contents of this page.	Can the child: • remember new information • locate information • read from left to right/return sweep?	Does the child locate and use resources in the room to answer some of the questions?

page 8

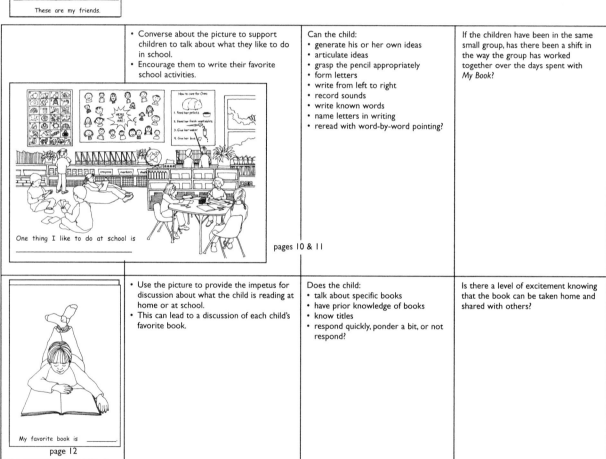

	• Read this page to the children (invite them to read with you). • Provide time to talk about their friends and draw their friends. • Invite the children to label their picture with friends' names. page 9	Can the child: • identify friends • select specific friends • draw friends (with some proportion and detail) • access friends' names in order to label?	Does the child talk with others in order to elicit information? ("How do you spell your name?")
These are my friends.			
	• Converse about the picture to support children to talk about what they like to do in school. • Encourage them to write their favorite school activities.	Can the child: • generate his or her own ideas • articulate ideas • grasp the pencil appropriately • form letters • write from left to right • record sounds • write known words • name letters in writing • reread with word-by-word pointing?	If the children have been in the same small group, has there been a shift in the way the group has worked together over the days spent with *My Book*?
One thing I like to do at school is _____	pages 10 & 11		
My favorite book is _____ page 12	• Use the picture to provide the impetus for discussion about what the child is reading at home or at school. • This can lead to a discussion of each child's favorite book.	Does the child: • talk about specific books • have prior knowledge of books • know titles • respond quickly, ponder a bit, or not respond?	Is there a level of excitement knowing that the book can be taken home and shared with others?

appendix b

MONITORING—LETTERS, SOUNDS, WORDS

Consonants and Diagraphs

	Date Letter Name	Letter Formation		Date Taught Sound	Date(s) Used	Date Maintained
		UC	LC			
b						
c						
d						
f						
g						
h						
j						
k						
l						
m						
n						
p						
qu						
r						
s						
t						
v						
w						
x						
y						
z						

ESSENTIAL WORDS

Date Taught	Date Maintained

Vowels

	Date Letter Name	Letter Formation		Date Sound Taught	Date(s) Used	Date Maintained
		UC	LC			
a at						
e end						
i it						
o on						
u up						

appendix c

MOONEY'S CHARACTERISTICS OF LEARNERS: EMERGENT AND EARLY 1

Emergent

Emergent and Early 1

Oral Language

- Replies on topic
- Answers a question
- Names/labels a noun, e.g., chair
- Greets and farewells a person
- Expresses a need with clarity
- Talks about or to people by name
- Listens attentively
- Follows and repeats instructions
- Looks at speaker
- Uses conversation conventions, e.g., excuse me
- Shows willingness to talk
- Takes turns
- Distinguishes between asking and telling sentences
- Knows the difference between reading voice and talking voice
- Uses appropriate ways of getting attention
- Retells a partner's words accurately
- Responds to body language
- Uses prepositions of place, e.g, by, before, between, beside
- Describes similarities and differences

Reading

- Holds book up the right way
- Shows awareness of directionality
- Knows where to look for the title
- Turns pages appropriately
- Distinguishes between front and back of book
- Uses letter sounds and names
- Knows capital and lower case letters
- Uses one-to-one matching consistently
- Understands function of spaces
- Identifies topic
- Knows the difference between word and letter
- Understands what a sentence is
- Knows 20 to 25 highfrequeiicy words
- Knows full stops (periods), capital letters, question mark
- Begins to self-correct
- Attends to initial letters when decoding
- Applies letter sounds when decoding
- Recognizes familiar parts within words
- Asks who, why, what, which, how, when questions

Written Language

- Creates story/picture match
- Holds pencillpen properly
- Follows conventional directionality
- Dictates a sentence for scribing
- Displays positive attitude to writing
- Make some letter/sound links—approximates using mainly consonants
- Includes spacing between words
- Moves toward writing on their own
- Forms letters correctly—knows and can differentiate between capitals and lowercase
- Locates and copies some basic vocabulary accurately
- Accurately uses writing vocabulary of 15 to 20 words
- Spells an increasing number of words accurately
- Shows confidence and enjoyment in expressing themselves

Visual Language

- Understands the way text works—spaces, front back, re-runs etc.
- Responds to images and presentation
- Creates images and presentation
- Enjoys reciting poems, rhymes, finger-plays
- Understands difference between photos and illustrations in a book
- Presents information in another form
- Understands symbols
- Understands that words and images can be combined to make meaning
- Presents for an audience

From Characteristics of Learners © 2004 by Margaret E. Mooney.

Early 1

Emergent and Early 1

Oral Language

- Uses different sentence starters in conversation
- Stays on topic more consistently
- Tells a simple event with beginning, middle, and end
- Talks about emotions
- Enunciates word endings
- Asks for assistance
- Follows sequence of instructions with some detail
- Speaks in an audible voice at an appropriate level
- Answers/replies in full sentences
- Recounts dialogue
- Makes inferences from peopleís body language
- Makes statements/asks questions
- Offers an apology with a statement of what they did wrong, e.g., sorry for hurting you

Reading

- Makes inferences from illustrations
- Doesn't always use the picture as the predictive cue
- Attends to final letter
- Does not always use finger pointing
- Copes with text above illustration as well as below
- Identifies main character
- Begins independent self-correction
- Attends to beginning, middle, and end of words
- Uses basic punctuation to chunk for meaning
- Answers inferential questions
- Retells a simple story of two or three incidents
- Locates words that tell the who, what, when, which, how words, and so on
- Uses phrasing, e.g., in the garden
- Knows about 50 sight words
- Recognizes and reads a bank of high-frequency words
- Knows and uses some common blends
- Identifies speaker and spoken text

Written Language

- Uses word sources— walls/familiar books
- Includes some adjectives
- Begins to use different sentence beginnings
- Re-reads writing to self for checking
- Follows space and directionality conventions consistently
- Uses a consonant framework, but also some vowels
- Applies correct letter formation
- Writes one sentence with an accurate picture match
- Working toward two good sentences that are linked in meaning
- Uses capital letters and full stops (periods)
- Shows automaticity of approximately 25 to 80 words
- Begins to revise work more frequently
- Forms letters in consistent size

Visual Language

- Understands the way text works—spaces, front, back, re-runs, etc.
- Responds to images and presentation
- Creates images and presentation
- Presents information in another form
- Understands symbols
- Understands that words and images can be combined to make meaning
- Presents for an audience
- Enjoys reciting poems, rhymes, finger-plays
- Understands difference between photos and illustrations in a book

appendix d

The Literacy Record

Child's Name _____ Date of Birth _____

DEVELOPMENT OF ATTITUDES	BEHAVIORS TO OBSERVE	DATE observed	repeated	established
Enjoys writing	Seeks involvement and becomes engaged			
Enjoys reading	Seeks involvement and becomes engaged			
Expects writing to make sense	Rereads to confirm meaning			
Enjoys rhyme and rhythm of language	Uses book language in retelling Uses book language in writing (Once upon a time ...)			
DEVELOPMENT OF ATTITUDES	**BEHAVIORS TO OBSERVE**	**DATE** observed	repeated	established
Front and back of book	Automatically starts at front of book (trade and own published books)			
Left to right and return sweep	Reads left to right with return sweep Writes left to right with return sweep			
Word-by-word matching	Can match finger, voice, print in trade and own books Articulates difference between a letter and a word			
Pictures as a source of information	Uses pictures in reading to prompt anticipation and prediction			
Structure of a story	Uses structure in writing			
Concept of a word	Has control over a number of words in writing and reading			
Letters of a word are written in a sequence	Recognizes, can read and write own name and some other words			
Features of text	Can identify and use some punctuation in reading and writing			
Speech sounds can be written as letters	Approximates spelling in writing using consistent sound/letter (Underline or highlight when student is consistent)	A B C D E F G H I J K L M N O P Q R S T U V W X Y Z a a b c d e f g g h i j k l m n o p q r s t u v w x y z		
Printed words have letters represented by sounds	Uses visual information to relate letter to initial sound in reading			
Letter form generalizations Upper- and lowercase letters	Uses letters of alphabet in writing Recognizes letters of alphabet (Underline or highlight when student is consistent)	A B C D E F G H I J K L M N O P Q R S T U V W X Y Z a a b c d e f g g h i j k l m n o p q r s t u v w x y z		

front

The Literacy Record

Child's Name _____ Date of Birth _____

DATE	TEXT	RECORD OF ORAL READING	SUMMARY STATEMENT
	SP TB	Title	
	SP TB	Title	
	SP TB	Title	
	SP TB	Title	
	SP TB	Title	
	SP TB	Title	
	SP TB	Title	

KEY   SP   **Student published**
            TB   **Trade book**

Available from Richard C. Owen Publishers, Inc.
PO Box 585 • Katonah, New York 10536 • Orders: 800-262-0787 • www.RCOwen.com
Created by Marilyn Duncan. © 2005 by Richard C. Owen Publishers, Inc. All rights reserved.

back

appendix e

ESSENTIAL WORDS FOR SPELLING AND WRITING

Name: _____ Date: _____

School: _____ Date of Birth: _____

A
a
about
after
again
all
also
always
am
an
and
another
any
are
around
as
asked
at
away

B
baby
back
bad
be
because
bed
been
before
being
best
big
bit
black
boat
bought
boy
brother
bus
but
buy
by

C
called
came
camp
can
car
cat
come
coming
cool
could

D
dad
dark
day
dead
decided
did
died
do
dog
doing
door
down

E
each
eat
end
even
ever
every
everyone
everything
eyes

F
face
family
fast
father
fell
felt
few
finally
find
finished
first
five
food
for
found
four
friend
from
fun

G
game
gave
get
getting
girl
go
going
gone
good
got

ground
guard

H
had
hand
happened
happy
has
have
head
heard
he
help
her
here
him
his
hit
hole
home
hot
hour
house
how

I
I
if
Iill
Iim
in
inside
into
as
it
its
itís

J
jump
just

K
knew
know

last
later
left
let
life
like
little
live
long
look

looked
lot
lunch

M
made
make
man
many
me
minutes
money
more
morning
most
mother
much
mum (mom)
my

N
name
never
new
next
nice
night
no
not
now

Q
of
off
old
on
once
one
only
open
opened
or
other
our
out
outside
over

P
parents
people
picked
place
play
playing
presents
put

Q
R
ran
read
ready
really
ride
right
road
room
run

S
said
sat
say
saw
school
sea
see
she
sleep
should
side
sister
small
so
some
something
sometimes
soon
stay
still
stop
suddenly
swimming

T
take
tea
tell
ten
than
that
there
they
thing
think
this
thought
three
through
time
to
told
too

took
top
town
tree
tried
turned
two

U
under
until
up
us

V
very

W
wait
walked
want
wanted
was
water
way
we
well
went
were
what
when
where
which
while
who
why
will
window
with
woke
won
work
worked
would

X

Y
year
yes
you
your

Z

The 290 words on the following list are the ones most often used by writers in New Zealand. They make up about three-quarters of most writing, so they are important. Classroom teachers in New Zealand do not teach to the list. The teacher of five year olds notes command of a word by the child (frequent correct spelling on writing samples) with one color of highlighter. The list stays in the child's folder and goes to the next teacher, who nots command of words with a different color highlighters. AS the folder moves from teacher to teacher [as noted at lower right of list], the number of unfamiliar words decreases. Teachers and parents can see growth in spelling proficiency without ever giving the child a spelling list.
Adapted from Croft, Cedric. *Spell-Write: An Aid to Writing and Spelling*. Wellington, New Zealand: New Zealand Council for Educational Research, 1998.

appendix f

Icons for Student Daily Plan

1—Writing

2—Reading

3—Spelling

4—Handwriting

5—Exploring Books

6—Computer

7—ABC Work

8—Listening

9—Big Books

10—Word Work

11—Poetry Book

12—Flannel Board

Icons for Student Daily Plan (*continued*)

13—Puppets 14—Drama 15—Storytelling

16—Publishing 17—Investigation

TEMPLATE FOR STUDENT PLANNING SHEET TO USE AT BEGINNING–MIDDLE OF YEAR

name: _____ date: / /

Monday   Tuesday   Wednesday   Thursday   Friday

reading	writing

TEMPLATE FOR STUDENT PLANNING SHEET TO USE AT MIDDLE–END OF YEAR

name: _____ date: __ / __ / __

Monday	Tuesday	Wednesday	Thursday	Friday
1	2	3	4	5	6	7	8

☐ ☐ reading

☐ ☐ writing

☐ ☐

☐ ☐

☐ ☐

☐ ☐

☐ ☐

☐ ☐

appendix g

MONTHLY PLAN

Literacy Planning for Month of: _____

READING/WRITING DEMONSTRATIONS

OUTCOME:	
READERS	**WRITERS**

SMALL GROUPS

INSTRUCTIONAL OBJECTIVE	GROUP	
	1	
	2	
	3	
	4	
	5	
	6	
	7	

INDIVIDUAL SKILLS/MONITORING LEARNING

3X OR MORE SKILL INSTRUCTION		DAILY INSTRUCTION	
STUDENTS	SKILLS	STUDENTS	SKILLS

MONITORING INDIVIDUAL APPLICATION

appendix h

WEEKLY PLAN

Week of:	MONDAY	TUESDAY	WEDNESDAY	THURSDAY	FRIDAY
SMALL GROUP INSTRUCTION Group Numbers					
DAILY PUBLISHING					
FOCUSED MONITORING Outcome:					
SPELLING					
ORAL READING RECORDS					

GROUP	STUDENT NAMES	INSTRUCTIONAL OBJECTIVE
1		
2		
3		
4		
5		
6		

appendix i

DAILY PLAN
For beginning-middle of year

Literacy Planning for Date: _____

WRITING DEMONSTRATION	READNG DEMONSTRATION	SONGS/POETRY
Obj:	Obj:	
Topic:	Text:	

Small Group Instruction

READING	READING	WRITING	ALPHABET
Obj:	Obj:	Obj:	Obj:
Group:	Group:	Group:	Group:
Resource:	Resource:	Resource:	Resource:

Publishing

NAME   TEACHING POINT

*Daily

Spelling

Oral Reading

Monitoring Learning
Focus:

Who?

NOTES

DAILY PLAN
For middle-end of year

Literacy Planning for Date: _____

WRITING DEMONSTRATION	READNG DEMONSTRATION	SONGS/POETRY
Obj:	Obj:	
Topic:	Text:	

Small Group Instruction

READING	READING	WRITING	WRITING
Obj:	Obj:	Obj:	Obj:
Group:	Group:	Group:	Group:
Resource:	Resource:	Resource:	Resource:

P u b l i s h i n g

NAME TEACHING POINT	Monitoring Learning
	Focus:
	Who:
	Focus:
	Who:
	Focus:
	Who:
	Focus:
	Who:

NOTES	Spelling	Oral Reading

Created by Marilyn Duncan. © 2005 Richard C. Owen Publishers, Inc. All rights reserved.

bibliography

Adams, Marilyn, J. 1990. *Beginning to Read: Thinking and Learning about Print.* Cambridge, MA: MIT Press.

Allington, Richard L. 2000. *What Really Matters for Struggling Readers: Designing Research Based Programs.* New York, NY: Longman.

Armbruster, Bonnie B., Fran Lehr, and Jean Osborn. 2001. *Put Reading First: The Research Building Blocks for Teaching Children to Read, Kindergarten Through Grade 3.* Jessup, MD: Partnership for Reading (National Institute for Literacy, National Institute of Child Health and Human Development, and U.S. Department of Education).

Ashton-Warner, Sylvia. 1980. *Teacher.* London: Virigo.

Boland, Janice. 1996. *The Fox.* Katonah, NY: Richard C. Owen Publishers, Inc.

Boland, Janice. 2001. *My Dog Fuzzy.* Katonah, NY: Richard C. Owen Publishers, Inc.

Boland, Janice. 1997. *The Pond.* Katonah, NY: Richard C. Owen Publishers, Inc.

Black, Paul and Dylan Wiliam. *Inside the Black Box: Raising Standards through Classroom Assessment.* London: King's College School of Education, 1998.

Black, Paul, Christine Harrison, Clare Lee, Behan Marshall, and Dylan Wiliam. 2003. *Assessment for Learning: Putting It into Practice.* Maidenhead: Open University Press.

Burningham, John. 1971. *Mr. Grumpy's Outing.* New York: NY: Henry Holt and Company.

Calkins, Lucy. 1986. *The Art of Teaching Writing.* Portsmouth, NH: Heinemann.

Cambourne, Brian. 1988. *The Whole Story: Natural Learning and the Acquisition of Literacy in the Classroom.* New Zealand: Ashton Scholastic.

Carlstrom, Nancy White. 1986. *Jesse Bear, What Will You Wear?* New York, NY: Simon and Schuster.

Cazden, Courtney. 1992. *Whole Language Plus: Essays on Literacy in the United States and New Zealand.* New York, NY: Teachers College Press.

Clay, Marie M. 1985. *The Early Detection of Reading Difficulties.* Portsmouth, NH: Heinemann.

Clay, Marie M. 1991. *Becoming Literate: The Construction of Inner Control.* Portsmouth, NH: Heinemann.

Clay, Marie M. 1998. *By Different Paths to Common Outcomes.* York, ME: Stenhouse.

Clay, Marie M. 2002. *An Observation Survey of Early Literacy Achievement,* 2nd Edition. Portsmouth, NH: Heinemann.

Cogan, Karen. 1999. *My Little Brother Ben.* Katonah, NY: Richard C. Owen Publishers, Inc.

Croft, Cedric. 1998. *Spell-Write: An Aid to Writing and Spelling,.* Wellington, New Zealand: New Zealand Council for Educational Research.

Crooks, Terry J. 1988. "The Impact of Classroom Evaluation Practices on Students." *Review of Educational Research.* Volume 58, pages 438-481.

Delpit, Lisa. 1995. *Other People's Children.* New York, NY: New Press.

Duncan, Isadora. 1928. *The Art of Dance.* Edited by Sheldon Cheney. New York: Mitchell Kennerly.

Duncan, Marilyn. 2005. *My Book.* Katonah, NY: Richard C. Owen Publishers, Inc.

Finney, Amy J. 2001. *Bedtime.* Katonah, NY: Richard C. Owen Publishers, Inc.

Hardin, Suzanne. 1999. *Dogs at School.* Katonah, NY: Richard C. Owen Publishers, Inc.

Hearne, Tina. 1981. *Care for Your Guinea Pig.* Glasgow and London: RCPCA.

Heath, Shirley B. 1983. *Ways with Words: Language, Life, and Work in Communities and Classrooms.* New York, NY: Cambridge University Press.

Holdaway, Don. 1979. *The Foundations of Literacy.* Sydney, NSW, Australia: Ashton Scholastic.

Holdaway, Don. 1980. *Independence in Reading.* Sydney, NSW, Australia: Ashton Scholastic.

Kamii, Constance, and Mary Ann Manning. 1999. "Before 'Invented' Spelling: Kindergartener's Awareness that Writing is Related to the Sounds of Speech." *Journal of Research in Childhood Education.* Volume 14, number 1, pages 16–25.

Malcolm, Margaret. 1996. *I Can Read.* Wellington, New Zealand: Learning Media for Ministry of Education.

Meek, Margaret. 1982. *Learning to Read.* London, England: The Bodley Head.

Ministry of Education. 1992. *Dancing with the Pen: The Learner as a Writer.* Wellington, New Zealand: Ministry of Education.

Ministry of Education. 1993. *New Zealand Curriculum Framework*. Wellington, New Zealand: Learning Media for Ministry of Education.

Mooney, Margaret E. 2004a. *A Book Is a Present: Selecting Text for Intentional Teaching*. Katonah, NY: Richard C. Owen Publishers, Inc.

Mooney, Margaret E. 2003. *Books for Young Learners Teacher Resource*. Katonah, NY: Richard C. Owen Publishers, Inc.

Mooney, Margaret E. 2004b. *Readers as Writers and Writers as Readers: Creating a Reading/Writing Folder*. Katonah, NY: Richard C. Owen Publishers, Inc.

Morrow, Lesley Mandel, Linda B. Gambrell, and Michael Pressley. 2003. *Best Practices in Literacy Instruction,* 2nd Edition. New York, NY: The Guilford Press.

Morrow, Lesley Mandel, Diane Tracey, Deborah Gee Woo, and Michael Pressley. 1999. "Characteristics of Exemplary First Grade Instruction." *The Reading Teacher*. Volume 52, pages 462–476.

Murray, Donald M. 1968. *A Writer Teaches Writing: A Practical Method of Teaching Composition*. Boston, MA: Houghton Mifflin.

National Association for the Education of Young Children. 1998. "A Joint Position Statement by NAEYC and International Reading Association: Learning to Read and Write: Developmentally Appropriate Practices for Young Children." *Young Children*. Volume 53, number 4, pages 30–46.

National Institute of Child Health and Human Development. 2000. Report of the National Reading Panel. Teaching Children to Read: An Evidence-Based Assessment of the Scientific Research Literature on Reading and Its Implications for Reading Instruction [Online]. Available: http://www.nichd.nih.gov/publications/nrp/smallbook.htm

Neuman, Susan B. and David K. Dickinson, editors. 2001. *Handbook of Early Literacy Research*. New York, NY: The Guilford Press.

Neuman, Susan B. 1998. "How Can We Enable All Children to Achieve?" In Susan B. Neuman and Kathy A. Roskos (Eds.), *Children Achieving: Best Practices in Early Literacy*. Newark, DE: International Reading Association, pages 18–32.

Neuman, Susan B. and Sue Bredekamp. 2000. "Becoming a Reader: A Developmentally Appropriate Approach." In Dorothy S. Strickland and Lesley Mandel Morrow (Eds.), *Beginning Reading and Writing*. Language and Literacy Series. Newark, DE: International Reading Association, pages 22–44.

Panofsky, Carolyn. 1994. "Developing the Representational Functions of Language." In Vera John-Steiner, Carolyn P. Panofsky, and Larry W. Smith (Eds.), *Sociocultural Approaches to Language and Literacy*. Cambridge, England: Cambridge University Press, pages 223–242.

Peek, Merle. 1988. *Mary Wore Her Red Dress and Henry Wore His Green Sneakers*. New York, NY: Clarion/Houghton Mifflin.

Pinnell, Gay S. and Irene C. Fountas. 2002. *Phonics Lessons: Letters, Words, and How They Work: Grade K.* Portsmouth, NH: FirstHand/ Heinemann.

Pressley, Michael, Joan Rankin, and Linda Yokoi. 1996. "A Survey of Instructional Practices of Primary Teachers Nominated as Effective in Promoting Literacy." *Elementary School Journal.* Volume 96, pages 363–384.

Richard C. Owen Publishers, Inc. 2004. *Literacy Learning: Teachers as Professional Decision Makers Resource Book.* Katonah, NY: Richard C. Owen Publishers, Inc.

Ruddell, Robert B. and Martha R. Ruddell. 1995. *Teaching Children to Read and Write: Becoming an Influential Teacher.* Boston, MA: Allyn and Bacon.

Schickedanz, Judith A. 1998. "What Is Developmentally Appropriate Practice in Early Literacy? Consider the Alphabet." In Susan B. Neuman and Kathy A. Roskos (Eds.), *Children Achieving: Best Practices in Early Literacy.* Newark, DE: International Reading Association, pages 20–37.

Slegers, Brenda. 1996. "A Review of the Research and Literature on Emergent Literacy." Urbana-Champaign, IL: ERIC Clearinghouse on Elementary and Early Childhood Education (ERIC Document Reproduction Service No. ED 397 959).

Sulzby, Elizabeth and William Teale. 1992. "Emergent Literacy." In Rebecca Barr, Michael L. Kamil, Peter Mosenthal, and P. David Pearson (Eds.), *Handbook of Reading Research,* Volume 2. New York, NY: Longman, pages 727–757.

Teale, William and Junko Yokota. 2000. "Beginning Reading and Writing: Perspectives on Instruction." In Dorothy S. Strickland and Lesley Mandel Morrow (Eds.), *Beginning Reading and Writing.* Language and Literacy Series. Newark, DE: International Reading Association, pages 3–21.

Tharp, Roland G. and Ronald Gallimore. 1993. *Rousing Minds to Life: Teaching, Learning, and Schooling in Social Context.* New York, NY: Cambridge University Press.

Vygotsky, Lev S. 1978. *Mind in Society: The Development of Psychological Processes.* Cambridge, MA: Harvard University Press.

Wells, Gordon. 1985. *The Meaning Makers: Children Learning Language and Using Language to Learn.* Portsmouth, NH: Heinemann.

Vernon-Feagans, Lynne. 1996. *Children's Talk in Communities and Classrooms: Understanding Children's Worlds.* Ames, IA: Blackwell Publishing.

Williams, Sue. 1996. *I Went Walking.* New York, NY: Red Wagon Books/Harcourt.

Wilson, Karma. 2003. *Bear Wants More.* New York, NY: Scholastic.

Wood, Audrey and Don Wood. 1984. *The Little Mouse, the Red Ripe Strawberry, and the Big Hungry Bear.* Swindon, England: Child's Play International Ltd.

Woodward, Virginia A., Jerome C. Harste, and Carolyn Burke. 1984. *Language Stories and Literacy Lessons.* Portsmouth, NH: Heinemann.

Index